BEIRUT:
FRONTLINE STORY

BEIRUT:
FRONTLINE STORY

Selim Nassib with Caroline Tisdall

Photographs by Chris Steele-Perkins

PLUTO  PRESS

First published in 1983 in Great Britain by Pluto Press Limited
The Works, 105a Torriano Avenue, London NW5 2RX
and simultaneously in the United States of America by
Africa World Press, P.O. Box 1892, Trenton, NJ 08608

Maps on pages 2, 26, 29 and 136 by David Turner
and on pages 140–41 by Swanston Graphics, Derby

Text designed by Claudine Meissner
Cover designed by Clive Challis GrR

Set by Wayside Graphics, Clevedon, Avon BS21 7JG

Printed in Great Britain by BAS Printers
Over Wallop, Stockbridge, Hampshire SO20 8JD
Bound by W. H. Ware & Son Limited, Tweed Road
Clevedon, Avon BS21 6QG

British Library Cataloguing in Publication Data
Nassib, Selim
    Beirut: frontline story.
    1. Beirut – Politics and government
    2. Beirut – History
    I. Title   II. Tisdall, Caroline
    III. Steele-Perkins, Chris
    956.92′044   DS89.B4

ISBN 0-86104-397-9

Cover photograph
Shattered memorial photograph of Palestinian youth
from Cemetery of the Martyrs, West Beirut

To the people of Sabra-Chatila and the other camps of Beirut

CONTENTS

PUBLISHER'S NOTE

Selim Nassib, a Lebanese journalist, was in Beirut as correspondent for the French daily, *Libération*, from June to August 1982. In making a selection from his dispatches (over eighty in all), we have given preference to those which describe the experiences of everyday life in the besieged city. 'The Pattern Repeats Itself', the chronology of the war, notes and interviews with survivors of the massacres are by Caroline Tisdall, journalist and film-maker, who has done much over the years through the *Guardian* newspaper to promote discussion of the Middle East and the Palestinian 'question'.

The pictures are by Chris Steele-Perkins, a freelance photographer with the Magnum agency who was in the Lebanon from 11 June to 14 July and 20 September to 5 October. They are a selection of his Lebanon photos, some of which have appeared in magazines and papers the world over. The photos and text form a complementary account of the summer of 1982.

Palestinian women in Sabra-Chatila camp with memorial photograph of a relative killed during the siege

THE PATTERN REPEATS ITSELF

CAROLINE TISDALL

'I found some bodies cold. Here the "cleaning up" had been done with machine guns, then hand grenades. It had been finished off with knives, anyone could see that. The same thing in the next room, but as I was about to leave, I heard a sigh. I looked everywhere, turned over all the bodies, and eventually found a little foot, still warm. It was a little girl of ten, mutilated by a hand grenade, but still alive . . . everywhere it was the same horrific sight.'

It could be an account of the massacre in the Palestinian refugee camp Sabra–Chatila in the summer of 1982. But it's another time, another place, another tragedy: the slaughter of 254 men, women and children in Deir Yassin, a village west of Jerusalem, on 10 April 1948. That day Jacques de Reynier, head of the International Red Cross in Palestine, encountered a detachment of Menachem Begin's Irgun Zvai Leumi in the village. They told him they were engaged in a 'cleaning up' operation. De Reynier's report to the International Red Cross continued: 'All of them were young, some even adolescent, men and women armed to the teeth; revolvers, machine guns, hand-grenades, and also cutlasses in their hands, most of them still bloodstained.'

Arnold Toynbee threw some light on the motivation for what was indeed neither the first nor the last of such massacres: 'I have heard, and no one denied what I have heard, that after one of these massacres, when all the civilians of all ages were slaughtered in Deir Yassin village west of Jerusalem, the Israeli armed forces toured around in jeeps announcing in Arabic through loudspeakers that "we have done this to the inhabitants of that place. So if you don't want us to do to you what we have done to them, then get out and leave your villages." '

They did – fleeing south to Gaza, east to Jordan and north to Lebanon. A land emptied of Palestinians was what Begin and the founding fathers of Israel wanted. In his autobiography *The Revolt* (London: W. H. Allen, 1951) Begin referred to the 'victory' of Deir Yassin: 'Arabs throughout the country, induced to believe wild tales of "Irgun butchery" were seized with limitless panic and started to flee for their lives. This mass flight soon developed into a maddened uncontrollable stampede.' A month later the state of Israel was declared, on land purged of many of its people.

It was no coincidence then that Begin himself mentioned Deir Yassin in connection with the 'cleaning up' of Palestinians in Lebanon. As David Shipler of the *New York Times* reported on 27 September 1982: 'It was Mr Begin himself who recalled Deir Yassin. He brought it up at a cabinet meeting and in several private conversations.' The similarities are striking: in both cases the massacre was committed by 'irregulars' (Irgun in 1948, the 13

Phalange and Haddad gangs in 1982) while the area was under the control of regular troops. Both massacres were planned to induce panic and flight. On both occasions Begin claimed to have known only later that the slaughter had taken place.

But it is too simple and too conveniently disingenuous to lay the blame only on Begin. 'Operation Peace in Galilee', which began the war in Lebanon, the siege of Beirut and the massacre of Sabra–Chatila, was not just the result of the fanaticism of Begin and military henchmen Ariel Sharon and Rafael Eitan. Rather it was the realisation of a long-held Israeli aspiration conceived by David Ben Gurion in 1948, elaborated by Moshe Dayan in 1955, and outlined in Washington by Ariel Sharon during his visit in May 1982, prior to the invasion.

In 1948, Ben Gurion, first prime minister of Israel, wrote in his diary that the multi-religious state of Lebanon should be overthrown and 'a Christian state ought to be set up there, with its southern frontier on the Litani.' The establishment of a neighbouring religious state would secure the safety of the theocratic state of Israel. That there would be no place for Palestinian refugees was also clear to Moshe Dayan: 'According to Dayan the only thing that's necessary is to find a Lebanese officer, even a major will do. We should either win his heart or buy him with money to declare himself the saviour of the Maronite population. Then the Israeli army will enter Lebanon, occupy the necessary territory and create a Christian regime that will ally itself with Israel. The territory from the Litani southwards will be totally annexed to Israel. Dayan recommends that this be done immediately, tomorrow.' (From the diary of the then Israeli foreign minister, Moshe Sharett.)

But 23 years passed, punctuated by wars with other Arab neighbours, and bombings and invasions of Lebanon, before this major was found, the renegade 'Major' Haddad whose 'Christian' militia was steadily built up and trained by Israel after the Lebanese civil war of 1975. It was then too that the Israeli government started to cultivate the Maronite Phalange Party, formed in 1936 after its founder Pierre Gemayel had visited Nazi Germany. The Phalangists too were sworn to 'rid our land of every single Palestinian' and 'Arab influence'. Strange alliances are formed in the name of national purity. Over the next seven years up to 1982, Begin, on his own admission, spent $100 million (some say $250 million) of his American military loans on the Phalangist militia's training and their armoury of tanks, artillery, ammunition, and even uniforms.

By 1978, the year after he became prime minister, Begin was confident enough to invade Lebanon. It was a full-scale onslaught with the green light from Washington since, for the United States, 'stability in the Middle East and the securing of Western interests' coincided with Israeli aspirations. Thousands of civilians were killed, scores of Lebanese villages destroyed, and at least a quarter of a million people in the south were made homeless and went north to join the refugees of 1948 and 1967 in Beirut. In spite of stiff local resistance and eventual withdrawal, world opinion had been muted: the West remained as indifferent to the deaths of thousands of Arab civilians as it had been to the pogroms of the Jews.

14   In 1982 Israel found a solid ally in Alexander Haig. During his visit to

Washington ten days before the invasion, Ariel Sharon had discussed Israel's plans with Haig and their common interest in Lebanon. Haig described it as 'a great strategic opportunity' and 'America's moment in the Middle East', an opportunity for the US to reconstitute Lebanon and rid it of the presence of 'an international terrorist organisation' in Beirut. In an interview with the *Jerusalem Post* Sharon said he had told Haig: 'We cannot live under the threat of Palestinian terrorism from Beirut. We do not see any alternative but to go there and clean up. We don't want you to be surprised.' (30 June 1982)

Whether or not Sharon briefed Haig on Israel's grander plans is not recorded, but as Jonathen Frankel, associate professor in the Hebrew University recorded in the *Jerusalem Post*: 'Ariel Sharon, after all, has never sought to keep secret his grand strategy, his three-pronged programme. Lebanon should be cleared of foreign forces (the PLO and the Syrians) and re-established as a Christian-dominated state. The PLO should be effectively destroyed; the occupied territories (West Bank and Gaza) annexed to Israel; their Arab population there granted a highly limited form of internal autonomy; and Jewish settlements vastly expanded. Finally, the Palestinians should be encouraged to overthrow the Hashemite kingdom, and convert Jordan into their own national state.' (27 June 1982)

The stage was set. As Gideon Hausner, former Attorney General, cabinet minister and prosecutor of Eichmann wrote in the *Jerusalem Post* in an article entitled 'Victory for Humanity': 'For the first time since the foundation of the Jewish state we were able to plan a campaign not as a result of foreign aggression as in 1948, 1967, 1973, and it was free of the restraints of embarrassing partners as in 1956. Israel has proved again its dedication, its power and its respect for human values.' (11 July 1982)

But who believed it? In Israel itself there were unprecedented demonstrations against the war, the loss of life and the scale of civilian casualties, and for the first time soldiers of the Israeli Defence Force were among the protestors. For the first time, too, placards appeared reminding Begin of Deir Yassin and of another massacre too: 'Down with Sharon – the butcher of Kibya', the West Bank village where, on the night of 14–15 October 1953, 69 people were murdered by Unit 101, led by the then Colonel Ariel Sharon, in reprisal for a Palestinian attack on the village of Yahoud in which a woman and two children were killed. By 23 September 1982 after the Sabra–Chatila massacre, an opinion poll conducted by the newspaper *Ha'aretz* showed that 80 per cent of Israelis felt the war had damaged them in the eyes of the world.

World opinion was indeed shocked by the carnage shown by television and newspapers. An optimistic Palestinian might even have been led to believe that the sacrifice of so many lives might at least lead to a fair hearing of four million survivors' case for a country of their own. But diplomatic duplicity continues. The PLO wrongly trusted the international community to defend its women and children when it evacuated Beirut. It wrongly hoped that the cynicism of the West would come to an end after the massacre. In the first week of December 1982 the US congress approved giving Israel $500 million more than President Reagan was asking for, in spite of protests from the State Department that this might give the wrong 15 signal to Tel Aviv. In the same week King Hassan of Morocco felt obliged to cancel talks between the British government and his seven-man Arab League delegation because the British prime minister Margaret Thatcher objected to the presence in that delegation of the PLO foreign affairs representative.

But world opinion had changed. Who would have expected to find the crews of American TV networks wearing teeshirts with the slogan 'I'm proud to live in Beirut West' while the city was besieged by the Israelis? Maybe this was the effect of a climate that was unique to the city. From the early seventies and then increasingly after the civil war of 1975–76, there were the beginnings of a non-sectarian society. In West Beirut and parts of the surrounding mountain areas and South Lebanon were to be found a mixture of races and creeds unimaginable in most parts of the world, let alone the sectarian Middle East envisaged by Zionist strategy. West Beirut was predominantly Moslem by faith, but becoming left-wing and revolutionary by experience. Within this *de facto* community of Lebanese, Palestinians, Syrian Jews and Armenians, there were Sunni and Shiite Moslems, Druze, Greek Orthodox Catholics and Maronite Christians, Islamic fundamentalists, Baathists, Nasserists, Marxists, and no doubt a few anarchists too. There were, of course, feuds and factions, sometimes shoot-outs and assassinations, of which much was made by the Western media. Very little was written about the day-to-day coexistence and tolerance in adversity that made this possible.

Access to people, particularly Palestinians, was easy in West Beirut and the areas of Lebanon where the PLO and the Lebanese National Movement were in control. Here, then, is another reason for Begin's determination to smash the PLO in Lebanon: ease of access meant more and more people were learning about the Palestinians and their history, either at first hand or through films, books and articles. In the eyes of the world, a human face had already been put to the 'two-legged animals', as Begin described the Palestinians when addressing the Knesset on 8 June 1982.

FROM AMMAN TO BEIRUT

European intellectuals and the left generally have not been keen to take up the question of Palestine. The reasons are many: a mixture of guilt and loyalty among an older generation, of ignorance or of failure to think through the ideological implications, of fear of being accused of being anti-semitic and/or having sympathy for 'terrorism'. There are exceptions like Noam Chomsky, who in many essays over the years has exposed the injustice done to the Palestinian people. In England, Erich Fried, the Austrian-born poet and refugee from the Nazis, has been publishing impassioned indictments since 1967:

When we were the persecuted
I was one of you
How can I remain one
when you become the persecutors?

Your longing was
to become like other nations
who murdered you
Now you have become like them

You have outlived
those who were cruel to you
Does their cruelty
live on in you now?

(from *Hear O Israel*, written in 1967)

In 1970, *La Comune*, the Milan theatre company of the writer and actor
Dario Fo, staged a comparison of the Italian and Palestinian resistance
movements, presenting history as a question: if the French and Italian
resistance to invasion and occupation are seen as historically correct and
heroic, why do Europeans use a double standard to condemn the Palestinians
for resisting?

That same year, Jean Genet visited the Palestinian camps and bases in
Jordan, just before King Hussein's Black September in which, according to
Palestinian figures, 22,500 fighters and civilians died at the hands of the
Jordanian Bedouin army. The parallels with Beirut 1982 are horrifying.

As an anti-nationalist, and an atheist, Genet went expecting to find
nationalism not revolutionary thinking, bigotry not tolerance, and embar-
rassment not indifference when, as he always does, he insisted on discussing
his homosexuality. He returned to write: 'A revolution which does not aim
at changing me by changing the relationships between people does not
interest me; what is more I doubt whether a revolution which does not affect
me enough to transform me is really a revolution at all. The Palestinian
revolution has established new kinds of relations which have changed me,
and in this sense the Palestinian revolution is my revolution.'

The things that affected Genet ranged from 'certain Palestinian women
whose looks disclosed such a vigour of mind, such an intellectual audacity'
to the spirit of the *fedayeen*. 'They had the gaiety of youth, the laughter, the
mischievousness you don't find in regular armies' and an awareness of
danger which 'made life in the bases something fine and austere.' Most of all
he was impressed by the quality which has been most overlooked in the
propaganda war to present the Palestinians as a 'lesser' people: 'What
comes to my mind first and foremost, and in the most delightful way, is the
commandos' great freedom of speech. The word "astonishing" is not too
strong to use here. They can talk of everything. I cannot recall that any
subject was taboo. They were utterly frank, whether they were criticising
authority, or religion as moral authority, or dealing with sexual problems.
. . . They were very intrigued by what was going on in China at that time,
and by Cuba. Everything was discussed, and discussed with a mixture of
gravity and humour.' (Jean Genet, 'The Palestinians', *Palestine Studies*, no.
9, Autumn 1973)

After the Black September massacres, Genet criticised the Palestinian
revolution for failing to establish links between the Palestinian and the 17

Jordanian masses and, thus, laying themselves open to defeat by Hussein. This criticism is over-simplified but it helps explain the efforts made by the PLO in Lebanon to establish a social and political infrastructure that reached beyond the camps and established links with the poorest and most oppressed sectors of Lebanese society. For Arab regimes, Israel and the West, such links are a menace, and here the parallels between what happened in Amman and Beirut form a pattern. From 1965 a younger generation of Palestinians, raised in the camps, flocked to join the PLO as fighters. In transforming camp identity from the abject humiliation of forgotten refugees into defiant strongholds of Palestinian nationalism, revolutionary thinking and military training, this generation also spawned new enemies. The governments and armies of Lebanon, Syria and Jordan, alarmed by Israeli reprisals for PLO raids and bombs in Israel, threatened by Palestinian radicalism and weakened by wars, clamped down on the PLO, the camps and the guerrillas. The Arabic word for this is *tahjim*: cutting down to size.

By 1970 Amman had become the headquarters of the PLO much as Beirut had become by 1982. Not only was Jordan threatened with Israeli reprisal but, with Palestinians forming 70 per cent of his population, King Hussein's authority was challenged by the PLO. There is little doubt that he had the support of the Western powers and Arab regimes to sort out the Palestinians in what has come to be known as Black September. This was when the surviving PLO officials and fighters moved headquarters to Beirut and Damascus. Many of the people from the refugee camps fled to Lebanon, joining the other 'post-1948' refugees as best they could. In the bitterness that followed came the Black September aeroplane hijackings, Munich, and deepened factionalism within the PLO as Georges Habash and the Popular Front for the Liberation of Palestine (PFLP) vented their rage and despair. How much greater must be the rage and despair after operations 'Peace in Galilee' and 'Iron Brain' (code name for the Sabra–Chatila operation)? After all the years of diplomatic activity, the observation of a ceasefire from July 1981, evacuation, the handing over of arms and the entrustment of the camps to the protection of an international peace-keeping force – what hope now in diplomacy?

For Arafat and the moderates within the PLO, the forced move to Lebanon was a turning point. It was from Beirut that Arafat went to the United Nations in 1974 with his offer of a gun or an olive branch, gaining the recognition of the PLO as 'the sole legitimate representative of the Palestinian people' from 115 countries and a statute of diplomatic status from the UN. It was to Beirut that politicians, diplomats and media people from all over the world came to find out more, and from Beirut that Arafat was welcomed not as the leader of a terrorist organisation but as an equal, even by some European heads of state.

Although fewer than 10 per cent (some 350,000 according to UNESCO figures) of the total Palestinian population were living in Lebanon before the summer of 1982, they had become the symbol of resistance and an inspiration to those living under occupation in Israel, the West Bank and Gaza. Up to the time of the civil war of 1975–76, most of them had been living in the 17 camps set up by the United Nations Relief Works Agency

(UNRWA) after 1948. Seven of these camps, again before the civil war, were in Beirut. Originally the camps were set up as temporary shelter, hence the insistence, still the official policy, of small one-storey buildings, open sewers and so on, since anything more elaborate comes to represent a permanent acceptance. Over the years some of the camps became more elaborate as families grew and the original 1948 refugees were joined by new victims. Only the original 1948 people were entitled to the meagre UNRWA monthly rations: ½ kilo of rice, 7 kilos of flour, ½ kilo of sugar and ½ litre of cooking oil. These are collected from ration posts within the camps on production of the 1948 UNRWA registration card. After the invasion of 1982 these symbols of abjection became crucial to survival. Without one you could get no food from rations posts manned by Israelis and Phalangists, and you ran the risk of being rounded up as a non-registered alien. At the same time, in the panic of Beirut people were tearing up their UNRWA cards for fear of betraying their identity as Palestinians.

In the early years the Lebanese government kept the refugees coralled in the camps. The internal balance of power was threatened by the influx of a predominantly Muslim population. The demographic issue is even more crucial now with the Phalangists back in power and already suggesting that, of the Palestinians surviving the war and the massacre, only 50,000 of the 1948 registered refugees should be allowed to live in Lebanon.

Thus from 1948 to 1969, when PLO organisation was established in the camps, the solution was to keep the Palestinians out of Lebanese life, out of the economy, unable to communicate between camps, and controlled by the Lebanese intelligence service, the Deuxième Bureau.

'Until this moment the camps had been stagnating. In most of them the population had more than doubled since 1948 and conditions were dreadful. We were overcrowded, we had no social or sporting facilities, our education and our health care were inadequate. Moreover we were under severe restrictions. We had to be in our homes every night at 6 p.m. We were forbidden to organise, only four or five people were allowed to meet together at any one time. It was necessary to obtain special permission even to form a gathering for a marriage. And on those occasions like May 15th [date of the establishment of the state of Israel] when we defied the authorities there were violent clashes between us. The end of the suppression was the start of the revolution.'

Haj Talal was among the PLO organisers who took over the camps from the Lebanese authorities in 1969. Fatah became responsible for guarding and discipline in the camps, and military training started. The Palestinian flag flew over the camps and people dared sing and dance in their own tradition. People's committees were set up to administer camp life and negotiate between individual refugees and the Lebanese authorities. Over the years the people's committees, working by democratic procedures, came to represent all the groups within the PLO. Consciousness-raising began: speeches, rallies and the radio of the resistance.

The camps are the most potent symbol of injustice but, after Jordan in 1970, the PLO began to build an infrastructure to counter the helpless waiting on foreign soil. In and around the camps, a network of services was set up to tackle the most demoralising aspects of exile – dependency on 19 others for work, medical care and education. The Samed ('steadfastness') workshops were started, initially to provide work for the sons and daughters of those who had died in Jordan, producing woodwork, metalwork, furnitures and the crafts and traditions which had been neglected since 1948. The low-level education offered by the UNRWA schools was supplemented by kindergartens and lessons in Palestinian history and culture. Research centres and printing presses started to document a lost history. Most ambitious of all was the building of hospitals and clinics throughout Lebanon by the Palestinian Red Crescent Society (PRCS) which set out in 1970 to put into practice what had been learned in Jordan. All the PRCS services, from preventative medicine to surgery and childcare, were offered to the Lebanese poor on a non-sectarian basis.

Political alliances were forged with the Lebanese too. In the early 1970s Kemal Jumblatt, leader of the secretive Druze sect which is 120,000 strong in the central Chouf mountains of Lebanon, formed the Arab Popular Front for the Support of the Palestinian Revolution, which later evolved into the Lebanese National Movement.

THE LESSONS OF THE CIVIL WAR

People say the Lebanese civil war of 1975–76 had no beginning and no end. Extremes and tensions were menacingly obvious the first time I was there, two years earlier. At that time the official image was one of pro-Western chic of the kind the Shah and Sadat favoured, too – lavish festivals of European and American culture and government tourist brochures which seemed ironic even then: 'Life is pleasant in Beirut, banking centre of the Mediterranean. Its lovely beaches are open most of the year, and its nightclubs – probably more to the square mile than in any other metropolis – provide entertainment both for the country's fun-loving, carefree inhabitants and for the visitors who, from the minute they step on Lebanese soil, feel the country's welcome.'

My welcome came from a charming French-educated government guide of 24 who cheerfully volunteered the information that she was a member of the Phalange Party. As we drove into Beirut she pointed out the first of the Palestinian camps behind the pine trees. 'Those animals,' she said 'are the disease of this country.' A few days later, having slipped the leash, I was staring at the victims of an Israeli shelling in the south Lebanon refugee camp at Nabatiyeh, which has since disappeared from the map. All around were shattered homes, yet the splendid house of a Lebanese minister just to the south was unscathed. 'What precision,' said the embittered survivor of Amman who accompanied me.

But nothing escaped unscathed in the hell of the 1975–76 civil war. There were 60,000 deaths and out of the street battles and massacres came the hatreds of today. According to the Palestinians, it started when the Phalangists attacked a bus full of Palestinians going to a wedding. Then came the battles and massacres. Most savagely attacked were the three Palestinian camps and the shanty towns housing non-Maronites which lay in what is now East Beirut. The camps of Dbayeh and Jasr al-Basha – inhabited mostly by Christian Palestinians – were the first to go, followed by the poor area of Dikwani. Then came the hideous slaughter in two quarters of West Beirut: Maslakh, where Kurds and Palestinians lived, and Karantina, where the homes of 10,000 people were razed to the ground as right-wing Christian militia 'cleansed' the city of a few thousand of its most vulnerable and impoverished inhabitants. Those who escaped the massacre fled to the beaches south of Beirut, to blocks of flats along the shore which were being abandoned by the Maronites as the country began to divide into north and south. The Palestinians retaliated in Damour and other Maronite villages along the strategic coast road just south of Beirut. Survivors were taken to boats and ferried northwards. (It is now widely believed that the Sabra–Chatila massacres were carried out by a Damouri brigade seeking revenge.)

There was worse to come. In East Beirut there still remained Tal al-Zaatar, a large camp housing 30,000 Palestinians. Unlike Karantina and Maslakh it was heavily defended, and came under siege in the spring of 1976. For months the shelling continued. Food, water and medicine were cut off, people were dying of starvation until on 12 August, the PLO, already overstretched fighting against the Syrians, ordered the camp to surrender. According to Dr Abdul Aziz Labadi's book *Diary of a Palestinian Doctor* an assurance was that day conveyed to the survivors by the leaders of the Phalange. It read, 'We guarantee that no one will harm you. We have agreed with your leadership to evacuate the camp of all civilians with the assistance of the International Red Cross.' As they came out, a thousand people – children, men and women – were butchered with a barbarism excessive even by Lebanese civil war standards. Those who survived the carnage were settled in Damour.

As Jonathan Dimbleby wrote in his book *The Palestinians* (London: Quartet, 1979): 'Those who have seen a baby garrotted, a husband tied between two vehicles facing in opposite directions and then torn in half as they accelerate away, or teenage boys lined up and "executed" by a firing squad, and little girls suffocated under the press of panic-stricken bodies that drove them to safety, do not quickly recover.' With a precedent like this who could doubt what fate awaited the inhabitants of Sabra–Chatila once they were left undefended and at the mercy of the Phalange?

The lessons of the civil war were bitter for the Palestinians. In the course of it they had been betrayed and duped not only by Israel and the United States, which was to be expected, but also by Syria, Iraq, Egypt and Saudi Arabia. Lebanon was shattered and divided: north–south, right–left, east–west. Vast quantities of capital and investment had been taken out of the country as the rich fled. Banking and tourism were dead too, so 70 per cent of the Maronite economic structure had disappeared. In West Beirut and south Lebanon, the Palestinians and the left took over the abandoned flats, villas and farm lands. Unhindered by Lebanese government control but under the watchful eye of the Syrian contingent of the Arab Deterrent Force, they began to restructure and fortify their revolution.

STEADFASTNESS AND REVOLUTION

'The Palestinian revolution is not just the fighter's gun. It is also the writer's pen, the surgeon's knife, the nurse's patience.' (Yasser Arafat)

From 1976 to the invasion of 1982, the PLO rebuilt and extended their infrastructure in Lebanon, attempting to create what Arafat described wryly as 'the microcosm of our future mini-state'. By June 1982 the Palestinian Red Crescent Society was treating almost a million cases a year in its network of nine hospitals and 12 clinics, and offered a full health service from ante-natal care to cardiac by-pass, 'regardless of race, colour, religion or political affiliation'. As a major social achievement it attracted many visitors, including foreign doctors and nurses from all over the world, some of whom were to become crucial witnesses to the massacre. Scandinavians were the most numerous volunteers, and Norwegian and Swedish clinics were opened in the refugee camps of the south. Now the Palestinian Red Crescent is wrecked, its buildings destroyed or taken over, leaving the people without doctors they can trust.

The Samed workshops expanded too, and with them the trade union movement. Visitors could discuss production and labour relations in 32 factories and workshops employing about 3,000 Palestinians and Lebanese men and women. Furniture was exported to Arab countries and the Eastern bloc. Boots, blankets and the traditional *kouffiyeh*, made world-famous by Arafat, were produced for the fighters in hillside buildings that had once belonged to Maronite industrialists. Some of the qualified Palestinians in diaspora returned to run the factories. Amin Izar, senior engineer of the blanket factory, became a familiar spokesman: 'The workshops and factories are the nucleus for a liberated Palestine. We do not work here for the sake of work, though unemployment runs at about 20 per cent in the camps. These machines are the arms of the Palestinian people . . . our production here is to build the human being, not profit. Our production reveals us to ourselves as people . . . The workers sit on the central planning, financing and marketing committees. Our industrial relations are drawn up on socialist lines, but we believe they could fit into a capitalist society.' Less diplomatically, a girl working a Jacquard loom said with a smile that ideological differences were kept for weekly discussion sessions: 'After all, among us there are workers from different groups within the PLO and not all of us would wish to fit in with a capitalist system!'

Workshops for the traditional crafts of Palestine were set up in all the camps. Each object produced was laden with history and geography which reflected the culture of the different towns and villages which made up Palestine: the mother of pearl work of Bethlehem, the olive wood carvings of Jerusalem, the glass blowing of Hebron. Palestinian cultural identity was proved by tracing each of these traditions back through the centuries. The propaganda of embroidery took on added significance when Moshe Dayan's wife set up Maskit, the Israeli craft bureau which exported traditional Palestinian dresses to Europe and the United States with 'made in Israel' labels added. The Samed workshops responded with a catalogue of over 200 designs systematically analysing each pattern and stitch design according to which village it came from and what each of the stylised shapes meant within a peasant Palestinian society: birds, hedgehogs, cows' eyes, flowerpots, signs of the Zodiac. As long as the relative peace lasted, this affirmation of Palestinian cultural identity flowered.

With the excuse of reprisal for *fedayeen* raids and shellings, Israel invaded the south again and again. Shelling from warships and F11 bombing raids along the coast and on West Beirut were so common that they were hardly ever mentioned in the Western press. One bombing attack I saw in 1979 happened along a 20-mile stretch of the coast road at 6 p.m. one Sunday when the traffic returning from a day's outing by the sea was particularly heavy. For 17 minutes the F11s dropped their bombs over the road and five villages. Twenty people were killed and 60 injured – none of them fighters. That night a military spokesman in Tel Aviv reported 'raids had been carried out on commando bases in south Lebanon'.

The most famous of these bases was Arnoun, or Beaufort Castle as the Crusaders had called it. You reached it by jeep from Nabatiyeh, across a few miles of bombed scorched earth, then scrambled up over the stones of its shallow northern side. Manning it were between 30 and 50 *fedayeen*, stationed there for about three months usually, with a day off now and then to visit their families. While I was there one of them, Jemil from Gaza, left to visit his wife who had just had their first child. In the rocky ground beneath the castle he was digging out the only present available: the tails of the bombs that had fallen around the men that day. 'For flower vases' he explained as he went off with a rope of them strung on his back. I don't think it was just a gesture for a visiting journalist.

The dug-outs inside the castle were small and quite cosy, benches covered with army blankets, an old field telephone, books and newspapers which became more precious as time ticked by. Sometimes the unit was a mixed group of Palestinians and Lebanese from different tendencies within the revolution. The strategic and emotional importance of the place only became clear if you ventured up onto the shattered ramparts, risking being sighted by the Haddad tanks 1,000 feet below and on the hillside to the east. Beyond and to the south was Galilee, so near and so far, accessible to these men only by the rockets they could fire into the kibbutzes and settlements which were once their fields and villages. Yet from here the Habib ceasefire of July 1981 was patiently observed for eleven months, in spite of three provocative Israeli incursions into Lebanon. It was the Israeli professor, Yehoshua Porath, who pointed out the terrible irony: 'I think the Israeli government's decision (or to be more exact, its two leaders' decision) resulted from the fact that the ceasefire had held . . . Yasser Arafat had succeeded in doing the impossible. He managed an indirect agreement, through American mediation, with Israel and even managed to keep it for a whole year . . . This was a disaster for Israel. If the PLO agreed upon and maintained a ceasefire they may in the future agree to a more far-reaching political settlement and maintain that too.' (*Ha'aretz*, 25 June 1982)

Selected Bibliography of Recent Publications:

— Bethell, Nicholas, *The Palestine Triangle — the Struggle between the British, the Jews and the Arabs, 1935 – 48*, London, Future Publications, 1980.

— Darwish, Mahmoud, *The Music of Human Flesh, Poems*, London and Washington D.C., Heinemann and Three Continents Press, 1981.

— Davis, Uri (ed) with Andrew Mack and Nera Yuval-Davis, *Israel and the Palestinians*, London, Ithaca Press, 1975.

— Dimbleby, Jonathan and McCullin, Don, *The Palestinians*, London, Melbourne & New York, Quartet Books, 1979.

— Gilmour, David, *The Dispossessed*, London, Sidgwick & Jackson, 1980.

— Flapan, Simha, *Zionism and the Palestinians* (to 1948), London, Croom Helm, 1969.

— Graham-Brown, Sarah, *Palestinians and their Society 1880 – 1946*, London, Melbourne & New York, Quartet Books, 1980.

— Hirst, David, *The Gun and the Olive Branch*, London, Faber, 1977.

— Jansen, Michael, *The Battle of Beirut*, London, Zed Press, 1982.

— Kanafani, Ghassan, *Men in the Sun*, short stories, trans. Hilary Kilpatrick, London & Washington D.C., Heinemann and Three Continents Press, 1978.

— Kayyali, A. W., *Palestine and Modern History*, London, Croom Helm, 1978.

— Langer, Felicia, *With My Own Eyes*, London, Ithaca Press, 1975.

— Said, Edward, *The Question of Palestine*, London & Henley, Routledge & Kegan Paul, 1980.

— Sayigh, Rosemary, *Palestinians: From Peasants to Revolutionaries* (with foreword by Noam Chomsky), London, Zed Press, 1979.

— Shehadeh, Rajah, *The Third Way: a Journal of Life in the West Bank*, London, Melbourne & New York, Quartet Books, 1982.

— Stewart, Desmond, *The Palestinians: Victims of Expediency (1980 – 81)*, London, Melbourne & New York, Quartet Books, 1982.

— Timerman, Jacobo, *The Longest War*, London, Picador, 1982.

— Turki, Fawaz, *The Disinherited, Journal of a Palestinian Exile*, New York & London, 2nd ed. Monthly Review Press, 1974.

Forthcoming:

— Smith, Pamela Ann, *Palestine and the Diaspora 1876 – 1982*, London, Croom Helm, June 1983.

Regular and indispensable:

— *Journal of Palestine Studies*, Washington D.C. & Kuwait, Institute for Palestine Studies and University of Kuwait, P.O. Box 19449, Washington D.C. 20036.

THE SIEGE OF BEIRUT

SELIM NASSIB

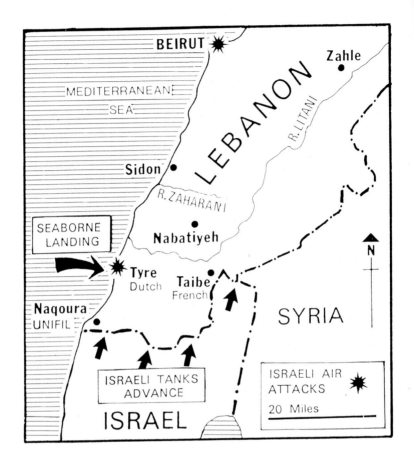

BEIRUT

Zahle

MEDITERRANEAN
SEA

LEBANON

R.LITANI

Sidon

R. ZAHARANI

SEABORNE
LANDING

Nabatiyeh

Tyre
Dutch

Taibe
French

Naqoura
UNIFIL

SYRIA

N

ISRAELI TANKS
ADVANCE

ISRAELI AIR
ATTACKS

20 Miles

ISRAEL

3 June:

Attempted assassination of Israeli ambassador to Britain, Shlomo Argov, shot outside the Dorchester Hotel. PLO denies all responsibility. After the detention of 4 Arabs (2 Jordanians, 1 Syrian, 1 Iraqi), Scotland Yard confirms that the PLO representative in London, Nabil Ramlawi, was target number 2 on the assassins' list.

4 June:

At 3.20 p.m. Israeli F15s, F16s and Phantoms start to bomb the predominantly Palestinian areas of West Beirut: Fakhani, which houses many of the PLO administrative offices; and the refugee camp Sabra–Chatila. Casualty figures in 50 raids estimated by the PLO to be 50 dead and 150 wounded, while Lebanese police figures give 210 dead and 250 wounded.

— PLO news agency WAFA claims Israeli action after Argov assassination attempt is 'just exploiting it before Philip Habib [US Middle East mediator] arrives.'

— PLO responds, 2 hours after bombings begin, with shelling of Northern Galilee and Haddad-held villages of south Lebanon. Twenty rockets hit Israeli towns and settlements in Galilee: 1 man dies of heart attack; 3 people wounded.

— PLO military leader Abu Jihad explains he had no choice but reluctantly to break the 11-month ceasefire negotiated by Habib in July 1981.

— Israeli radio reports relatively weak anti-aircraft fire and no Syrian intervention.

— Israeli foreign minister Yitzhak Shamir calls for complete elimination of PLO.

5 June:

Israeli offensive broadens to strike at 50 localities in 3 main areas: the Palestinian-dominated coast running from the southern suburbs of Beirut to Tyre in south Lebanon; the inland central section round Nabatiyeh and Beaufort Castle (Arnoun) 6 miles from the Galilee border; and the original 'Fatahland' – the south-eastern province of Arkoub in the shadow of Mount Hermon.

— Casualties put at 150 by PLO and Lebanese police: 75 civilians die in bombings of the coastal road; 20 children killed in bus just south of Beirut airport.

— UN Security Council vote 15–0 calling for immediate ceasefire.

— Alexander Haig, US secretary of state, at the Versailles economic summit of Western heads of state calls the situation 'very serious and one we regret tremendously.' Washington, he says, is making 'extensive diplomatic efforts to reinstate ceasefire'.

27

6 June:

Israel launches full-scale invasion of Lebanon by land, sea and air. The alleged objective of 'Operation Peace in Galilee' is to push the PLO back 40km from the Israeli border. Sidon, Tyre, Beaufort Castle, Nabatiyeh and Kawkaba (beyond the United Nations International Forces in Lebanon (UNIFIL) peacekeeping line) are besieged on a 50km front from the port of Tyre eastward to the hills of Mount Hermon. PLO resists in all targets while, on the eastern front, Syrians exchange fire. Israeli radio announces the invasion is not aimed at Syrians and will not engage with Syrian units unless attacked by them.

— A senior UN official at Naqoura watches the invasion convoy drive by: 'I have never seen so much armour and so many men in my life,' he said. 'But they were using a hammer to smash a wine glass. It was as if the Israelis were on military manoeuvres. They had tanks, personnel carriers and guns strung out bumper-to-bumper along the coast road here for more than 8 miles. One Syrian plane, just one, would have killed dozens of soldiers. But there were no planes.' (*The Times*, 6 July)

— Estimated Israeli invasion force: 25,000 troops stationed on border since February 1982, rising to 90,000 by 14 June. Total number of men under arms 172,000, later rising to 400,000 when reservists called up.

— Estimated PLO force in south Lebanon (according to *Jerusalem Post*, 7 June): 'PLO forces in southern Lebanon number 6,000 armed men, about half the PLO's total strength in Lebanon. According to Israeli military sources the terrorist concentrations include a string of heavily fortified positions each housing a platoon-strength force [20–30 men]. Only a few of the terrorist positions are in villages.'

— Massive bombings of Sidon, Tyre and Nabatiyeh and the refugee camps of Ain al-Helweh, al-Bas, Bourj al-Shemali and Rachidiyeh. Casualty figures may never be known. Estimates vary wildly from 15,000 (Lebanese prime minister Chafik Wazzan) through 10,000 (Lebanese police records) to 360 civilians and between 1,000 and 2,000 PLO fighters (Israel).

— At the end of the Versailles summit, US President Reagan refuses to deplore or condemn Israel for the invasion. His statement simply urges 'restraint' by all parties and deplores 'increasing bloodshed in that region'. British prime minister Margaret Thatcher agrees that 'The Middle East is a very, very considerable cause of real worry.'

Main Groups within the Palestine Liberation Organisation (PLO)

Fatah (Palestine National Liberation Movement) founded by Arafat 1958.

PFLP (Popular Front for the Liberation of Palestine) founded 1967–68 by Dr Georges Habash. Marxist.

PDFLP (Popular Democratic Front for the Liberation of Palestine) founded 1969 by Nayif Hawatmeh out of the PFLP. Marxist-Leninist.

PSF (Popular Struggle Front) split of PDFLP. Marxist-Leninist.

PFLP–GC (Popular Front for the Liberation of Palestine–General Command) founded by Ahmad Jibril out of the PFLP.

PLF (Palestine Liberation Front) split out of PFLP–GC.

Saiqa (Vanguards of the Popular Liberation War) founded 1968 as the Syrian wing.

ALF (Arab Liberation Front) founded 1969 as the Iraqi wing.

Main Institutions of the PLO

The Palestine National Council is composed of representatives of all groups, trade unions and independents (chairman: Khalid al-Fahoum). Every two years it elects the *Executive Committee* which is the equivalent of a cabinet. Its chairman is Yasser Arafat. *The Palestine National Fund* raises money from the Arab regimes (chairman: Dr Salah Dabbagh).

7 June:

Tyre and Nabatiyeh fall. Beaufort Castle captured. Defended by 30–50 Palestinians, it is taken only after a day and night of F16 bombing, then hours of fighting followed by hand-to-hand combat. The taking of the 'impregnable' Crusader fortress is hailed as major victory by Begin who flies in by helicopter as the Star of David is raised alongside the cedar-tree flag of 'Major' Haddad's 'Free Lebanon' zone. 'Beaufort is yours,' he says to Haddad. As former Israeli foreign minister Abba Eban remarked, 'It reminded me of Disraeli presenting India to Queen Victoria.'
— Bombings of Tyre, Sidon and Beirut continue, reinforced with shelling from warships. Exchanges with Syria limited to lower Bekaa plain. By nightfall Israeli troops are 30km south of Beirut.

8 June:

Sidon falls.

— Israel attacks Syrian Sam 6 missiles in eastern Bekaa. Syria brings in reinforcements for its 30,000 strong force. Habib arrives in Damascus from Israel for talks with Syrian leaders.
— Israel claims losses to date of 32 dead and 150 wounded.
— 500,000 people in an area covering a quarter of Lebanon now under Israeli occupation.

9 June:

Damour falls. Israelis invite original Maronite inhabitants to return. The encirclement of Beirut begins as Israel enters Khalde, 4km south of the city, near the airport.
— US vetoes UN Security Council resolution condemning Israel for refusing to withdraw forces and threatening Israel with sanctions.

10 June:

Israeli army's northern front commander, Brigadier General Amir Drouri: 'In a short time we will capture the city.'
— PLO newsreader: 'The enemy is bombing our camps, our women, our children. But we shall fight, fight, fight.'

Key Dates for the PLO

1958 Yasser Arafat founds Fatah (Palestine National Liberation Movement).

1964 Palestine Liberation Organisation founded by the Arab League in Cairo with Ahmed al-Choukeiry as chairman and a traditional army, the Palestine Liberation Army (PLA), with a contingent in each of the Arab states.

1965 First armed raid by Fatah in Israel.

1969 Arafat replaces Choukeiry as chairman of the executive committee of the PLO.

1974 Arab summit conference at Rabat recognises the PLO as the sole legitimate representative of the Palestinian people. Arafat addresses UN, which reaffirms the inalienable rights of the Palestinian people in Palestine.

1978 PLO bypassed by Camp David Agreement between US, Israel and Egypt.

1979 Arafat makes official visits to Austria, Spain and Turkey.

Thursday, 10 June 1982:
BEIRUT AWAITS THE ONSLAUGHT

The streets of the capital empty in almost an instant. It is midday. People vanish from the pavements, traffic disappears, shops close. West Beirut suddenly becomes a ghost town. Yet the weather is still fine, the sky still the same amazing blue of a moment ago. The difference is that the Israeli jets are on their way. You know they are coming by the noise. The Beirut airport is closed, so it can't be anything else. From behind shutters straining eyes try to make them out. You can see the planes swooping on Fakhani: the answering little puffs of white smoke from the anti-aircraft batteries are virtually useless against them. As a young Palestinian militant told me: 'What do you expect? Our Arab brothers have decided that we don't deserve better weapons . . .' The aircraft swoop and then soar, trailing regularly spaced decoy flares, to draw the anti-aircraft fire.

At the same moment, a wave of explosions rocks the capital. They have dropped another load of bombs. Columns of black smoke rise over the bombed section of the city. The sky darkens. But by this time the aircraft are far away, and the ragged rattle of gunfire that had greeted them stops. The silent deserted city holds its breath. A moment passes. The transistor radio gives details of the raid: the Palestinian camp of Sabra–Chatila has been hit; so were Fakhani (the West Beirut area that houses most of the PLO's offices), and the seafront areas of Ouzai and Khalde near the airport. Some bombs also fell near the UNESCO and Basta buildings.

The planes are already on their way back. The noon raid on West Beirut and the southern suburbs is the longest and fiercest attack since hostilities began. There are dozens of dead and wounded. Several areas of the city are burning. All members of the civil defence are mobilised. Ambulances are constantly ferrying people off to the city's overflowing hospitals.

Ever since last night, the same question has been on everyone's lips: are the Israelis going to invade the capital, or will they be content to lay siege to it, bomb it and strangle its lifelines? Beirutis are beginning to work out the odds for survival; obviously, the further you live from where the Palestinians are concentrated, the safer you are. Those are the areas that get bombed.

Everyone has their own little scenario. One bystander declares: 'They will never dare to attack Beirut. Several thousand Kalashnikovs are waiting for them here, and it would cost them too dearly.' Another says: 'They'll settle for cutting West Beirut in two, isolating the Palestinian and progressive areas from the rest.' A third suggests that: 'Begin has now gone so far that he can't really stop.' So the chorus of speculation carries on, now to the accompanying music of the bombing raids, which have started again.

After a bombardment in Fakhani, West Beirut

A serious threat or psychological warfare?

A serious threat? Or psychological warfare? The Israelis have air-dropped leaflets all over Beirut, calling on the Syrians to leave. After the latest drop, the little yellow leaflets are in everybody's hands.

On one side of the leaflet is a letter, written in Arabic, addressed personally to the commander of the Syrian troops still in the Lebanese capital. It is signed by the Israeli commander. A man-to-man sort of letter: basically Israel has such superior firepower at her disposal that any resistance would be pointless. You, sir, are responsible for the lives of your men, who have left wives and children back in their home country. So why embark on a battle that you have already lost? We are so very much stronger than you that nobody could accuse you of cowardice. Evacuate your positions quickly and you will have nothing to worry about. On the back of the leaflet is printed a map of Beirut and its suburbs, indicating to the Syrians the various escape routes that will be available to them should they decide to leave soon . . .

The Syrian choice: unequal battle or humiliating retreat

Israel is leaving the Syrians no other choice but to join battle or make a humiliating retreat. The day before, Wednesday, there were major air battles in the sky over the Bekaa valley. The Syrians are said to have lost 22 Migs – and also 7 batteries of their famous Sam 6 missiles. Syrian troops withdraw, without a fight, to the Beirut–Damascus highway in the north and to the ridge of Mount Lebanon to the east, where they set up fresh positions. They are aiming to defend the Dahr al-Baidar hill which guards the entrance to the Bekaa valley and the Syrian territory beyond it. By Thursday, the artillery duels on this front seem to have stopped. Instead the Israelis continue harassing the Syrian positions at Ahmur, Sahmur and Machghara in south-east Lebanon, presumably because these areas fall within the 40-kilometre limit that is Begin's declared *cordon sanitaire* for southern Lebanon.

But in Beirut hardly anybody believes any longer in this notional limit. Most of the Israeli forces have already crossed the Zahrani river and then driven on into the heart of the country, attacking and shelling two of its principal cities. This is how they have forced the Syrians to choose between retreat or battle.

This spectacular advance has indeed altered many things. At first, the Syrians found themselves obliged to take a stand (they could hardly have permitted themselves to be quietly shown the door). Later, though, the attitude of those living in the Palestinian and progressive areas began to alter. Before the Israeli invasion, many people had felt that both the Palestinians and the Syrians had gone too far. There had been a series of clashes and pitched battles between Shiites and Palestinian and progressive forces (south Lebanon, Chiah), and between Sunnis and Syrians (Tripoli). If Begin had stuck to his scenario of the 40-kilometre limit, perhaps this state of affairs would have continued. But the presence of the Israeli army at Deir al-Qamar, outside Aley and on the outskirts of Beirut – as well as the bitter resistance to the Israelis by the Palestinians – has begun to change all this.

Any one of the many groups who possess a rocket launcher (and there are several thousands of these weapons on hand) may decide to 'take out' an Israeli tank. Obviously, there are few illusions about the final outcome of any eventual battle. But, at the same time, days after the invasion began, it is clear that it has not been a walkover for the Israelis.

Massive mobilisation in Beirut

In West Beirut itself, the mobilisation is massive. At noon today, Thursday, at the very moment of the Israeli bombing, a Lebanese army detachment was moving into position on the Corniche al-Mazraa which runs along the seafront facing the Israeli warships. They were welcomed with open arms by the Palestinian and progressive forces stationed there.

In more general terms, all the young combatants who have been itching to fight at last find themselves face to face with a well-defined enemy. Anyway, the naval blockade, the closing of the Beirut–Damascus highway and the shutting of the airport have not left much choice. Those who are scared are either leaving or going to ground. With the Syrians gone from the capital, the *fedayeen* once again find themselves masters of the city. To regain their lost popularity, they have only to fight.

In order to raise morale, the fighters remember that the Israelis are trying to occupy a country that is mountainous, heavily populated, and under arms, with a Syrian army that cannot retreat, and a Palestinian and progressive front enjoying a new-found strength. How on earth can the Israelis hope to settle the matter, let alone settle it quickly? Beirut is bristling with Kalashnikovs, they say, not exactly a sitting target.

An invasion not wholly unwelcome

Obviously, not everyone in the capital shares this point of view. 'We're fairly happy with what's happening,' I was informed by the taxi driver who came from Jouniye to pick us up at the quayside. The *Sea Victory* was the first ship to reach the 'Christian' port since the airport was closed to traffic on 7 June. It was chartered by 14 journalists ready to pay whatever was necessary to get down to work right away; hence the presence of four or five taxi drivers who had spotted a good deal in the offing.

'Who else is going to rid us of the Syrians and Palestinians? We can't do it ourselves, and so . . .' Hearsay and idle conversation both indicate that the Christian population seems to favour the Israeli invasion. A preference that is not exactly shouted from the rooftops: it is a more discreet sympathy, at least up until now. But it is certainly there. For example, the Phalange radio makes much of its objective reporting – but it managed to announce the fall of Tyre, Sidon and Damour well before they actually happened. It also announced the death of Abu Jihad, Fatah's military leader, the day after the Israelis invaded. They stated that 'his body has been transferred to the morgue in the American Hospital.' The news was false – but a half hour later, Radio Israel also reported it, without attributing it to Phalange radio.

Bashir Gemayel, leader of the right-wing Christians, nonetheless takes great pains not to appear as a puppet of the Israelis. He has launched an appeal for discussions on a new Lebanese consensus, and for the formation of a government of national unity. Today, though, West Beirut regards Gemayel as a collaborator. The old splits of the civil war have re-emerged with surprising vigour.

French 'even-handedness'

It has taken six days for the Israeli army to reach the outskirts of Beirut. It has also taken six days for world diplomatic opinion to begin to make itself heard. Much hope has been pinned on the visit by the Saudi minister of foreign affairs, Prince Saud al-Faisal, to Bonn where he is to meet with Reagan, Mitterrand, Chancellor Schmidt and Margaret Thatcher. There is also favourable talk of the letter Reagan sent to Begin on Wednesday night, calling for an immediate ceasefire. But, after Mitterrand's heartening initial condemnation of Israeli aggression, came his later remarks, that Lebanon 'has already been occupied by two foreign armies' – a chilly qualification.

Still, the flurry of diplomatic activity, plus high-level contact between Washington and Moscow, suggests that, from now on, the Israelis will be pressed for time. Perhaps this means that tonight is going to be even worse for the people of Beirut than last night (when they were woken by Israeli shelling at four in the morning). But at least it is no longer a matter of 'resisting beyond the bounds of good sense'. Rather, it's a question of resisting until such point as the world imposes a ceasefire on Begin.

(Beirut, 10 June 1982)

Thursday, 10 June 1982: REFUGEES CONVERGE ON THE BEIRUT CITY CENTRE

The scene is the city's only public park. Its total area cannot be more than a couple of acres, with a large fish-pond in the middle. Before, there used to be portly park keepers watching over the lawns and flowerbeds, and young children from the area would come and ride their tricycles here.

But today the scene is different. Chased out by the bombing, West Beirut's refugees are shifting to the city centre, looking for makeshift accommodation in abandoned flats or in the open air. The lawns have tents pitched on them. The occupants of these tents, with their food, their transistor radios and their young children, have fled from the main areas under Israeli attack. For the umpteenth time they have packed up bundles of clothes, mattresses and a few cooking utensils, and have arrived in the city centre looking for shelter. There is no shortage of empty apartments, particularly in West Beirut itself where the war has driven out anyone with the money and means to leave. But it is not an easy matter breaking into
36 other people's houses. Heavy duty grills have been put across the entrances

to apartment blocks; muscular doormen have been hired; and many people have moved friends into their flats to look after them in their absence.

The number of refugees grows a little larger every day. Those who have relations in the city seek out the militia of the left-wing party favoured by their family. It is not uncommon to see a refugee family, escorted by armed militia, looking for a place to stay for the night, or for the week, or perhaps forever.

These wanderers from south Lebanon have already suffered a lot. Now they find themselves forced to break down doors and move into the houses of total strangers. Obviously, things are never that simple. It often happens that militias-accompanying-refugees clash with militias-defending-apartments – which then provokes the wrath of passers-by: 'So, while the Israelis are attacking us, you're going to spend your time fighting each other in a neighbourhood squabble?!'

But it is by helping people in need that the Palestinian and progressive forces have built their popularity. Other refugees, less in the know, have been forced to take refuge in the doorway of an apartment block, or a yard, or on a piece of wasteland. Some of them had even set up home on the wide flowerbeds running along either side of the al-Mazraa coast road. But, since the fighters were expecting an Israeli sea-landing at any moment, they decided to move on.

In fact, nowhere in West Beirut is particularly safe at this moment. Some people are leaving town altogether, with their bundles over their shoulders, to go God knows where. For those who have settled on the lawns of the public park, there is one small consolation: not only the greenery but a refreshment stall nearby which sells sweets for the children. And then, nobody is likely to bother them. It is, after all, as its name indicates, a public garden.

(Beirut, 10 June 1982)

Friday, 11 June 1982:
A BOMBING RAID ON THE CAPITAL

The explosions hit us without warning. We are thrown sprawling to the ground. Again, a whistling, and another explosion. Forty metres further on, down on the beach, there's a flash and a blast of heat. I try to hide behind a bush on the grassy central reservation of the main road. It's not wonderful protection. Our taxi driver is also crouching behind a bush, a kind of dwarf palm. Are we going to make a run for the side of the road? Or would it be better to wait a moment? Here comes that whistling noise again, another falling bomb. It is 2.35 in the afternoon, and the ceasefire called by the Israelis came into force at noon today! You must be kidding! You don't even have time to be afraid, really. Just a very powerful sense of stimulation, a kind of intense excitement, and the feeling that your mouth has completely dried up.

Our driver finally makes up his mind. Crouching low, he sets off at a run. I

Estimate of Israeli war machine deployed in Lebanon 1,300 tanks, 12,000 troop and supply trucks, 1,300 armoured personnel carriers, 350 ambulances and 300 buses to carry prisoners.

US military aid since 1948 $14.9 billion plus $7.15 billion in economic aid.

US supplies 85 per cent of Israel's planes including 120 F15s and F16s, plus the supersensitive electronics for the Sidewinder and Shrike missiles, and the Hawkeye surveillance and battle-controlled planes which can track up to 300 enemy aircraft 250 miles away. Israel was thus able to shoot down 79 Syrian aircraft, while losing only one of their own.

US-supplied bombs include cluster bombs, phosphorous bombs and shells, and possibly the vacuum bombs, terror weapons banned by the Geneva convention and as yet untested by the US in combat. As Israeli journalist Uri Avneri puts it: 'If Israel did not exist the American industrial complex would have to invent it.' (*New Outlook*, June–July 1982)

Weapons found in the PLO arsenals (according to Ze'ev Schiff, military corres- pondent of *Ha'aretz*): 'The only weapons found in large quantities were different types of rifles: some 10,000 Kalashnikov assault rifles' and (according to Hirsch Goodman): '51 heavy guns were captured including 2 old French 155mm guns and 32 Russian 130mm guns, and 240 other types of artillery, some of which could have belonged to the Syrians. The booty was also poor in Katushya rockets: of the 26 captured only 15 were the latest type . . . Did these arms threaten Israel's existence?' (*Jerusalem Post*, 9 July)

This certainly puts a more sober perspective on the accounts of captured Palestinian arsenals given by senior Israeli army officials to a shocked world in the second week of the war. They claimed that enough arms had been seized to equip a million 'terrorists', to a value of $5 billion, while ambassador-at-large Shabtai Rosenne, in a letter to *The Times* on 2 July described the hoard as sufficient to take 80 lorries a whole month to transport 4,000 tonnes of ammunition, plus 140 tanks and other military vehicles, 12,500 rifles and 520 heavy guns.

follow after him, running, and hurl myself down a slope leading down towards a half-built apartment block. Two fresh deafening explosions. We cover our heads with our hands. We'd do better to keep our heads right down. On the other side of the road the big dipper of a fair: it has somehow not been destroyed.

A few minutes of silence. All you hear is the distant rattle of Kalashnikovs and firing artillery. The soldiers on this front line tell us that there is fighting in a village about a kilometre further down the road.

Palestinian family with portrait of Yasser Arafat, West Beirut

They're bound to start firing

Our driver gets up again and sprints down the slope leading to the basement of the apartment block. In among the concrete pillars we find the rest of our team: the TV camera-operator, who has dropped his camera in the panic and is trying to find out if it still works; the correspondent from *Le Point*, who has a scratch across his forehead; four or five other journalists; the driver of the second taxi; and three soldiers belonging to the Shiite Amal movement. The shelling maintains its intensity. Those who know about these things claim that they must be using Milan ground-to-ground missiles. There is artillery fire too.

Our driver curses himself for leaving his car – a white American one – in the lane of traffic leaving Beirut. He's going to have to turn it round before heading back.

We decide to make a move. There's been no firing for five minutes now. We get to the foot of the slope. No chance! A small army truck heavily camouflaged with branches appears at the edge of the road. If the Israelis see it – and see it they most assuredly will – they're bound to start firing at it. We've just about worked out this proposition in our brains when once again the shells start whistling overhead. About turn! At the double!

We get back to the shelter of the apartment block. The lorry does a skidding turn and heads off towards Beirut. We wait. Nothing happens. Right – let's go. We run for it. The driver has already turned the car round. We pile in. A hundred yards further on we see our colleagues running out from the roadside clutching their gear. The car barely stops as we pick them up, and we're off down the road, like some gangster movie, with the doors still open.

In the 20 minutes before the noon ceasefire, Beirut was heavily bombed by Israeli planes. They come over either singly or in twos. From the tops of apartments in the city you can watch this aerial ballet at leisure. You don't actually see the bombs that they drop – only their results on the ground. The planes are bombing Fakhani, Sabra, Basta – the Palestinian and progressive areas of the capital. Columns of smoke rise from several different parts of town, blacking out whole patches of sky. Everyone thinks this is to show their military superiority at the moment of the ceasefire.

Rubble and broken glass

We run into small groups of soldiers all along the four kilometres of highway that run between the southern exit from Beirut and the front line at Khalde. The first group that stops us belongs to the Saiqa, the Palestinian organisation allied to Syria; the second are the Palestine Liberation Army (PLA); and the third group belong to the Shiite Amal movement. The PLA make problems for us, at first trying to turn us back. But when we insist, they decide to let us pass – at the same time warning our driver to watch out for small, white, V-shaped objects like clothes pegs: 'Don't drive over them – they're anti-personnel mines laid by the Israelis.' Needless to say, from that moment all the occupants of the car keep their eyes glued to the road ahead.

On both sides of the road we see the effects of the aerial, land and sea
bombardment – houses collapsed in a heap of rubble, broken glass, mounds

of masonry, and bomb craters three metres wide.

Eight days ago this area was packed with people; now there's not a soul to be seen. On the left, running parallel with the road, are the airport runways, guarded by dozens of men armed with Kalashnikovs. Beyond the airport loom the hills. We see puffs of white smoke appearing at regular intervals. The sound comes some time afterwards. Gunfire. The ceasefire is supposed to have been in operation for two hours now. The driver identifies for us the places that are being shelled: Brichmoun, Keyfoun and Bchemoun. We reach the crossing with the old Sidon road. Eight hours ago, this was the most southerly position held by the Syrians along the coast road. On the left we see the forest of radio masts of Radio Orient (which serves, among other things, to transmit the telex services that we ourselves are using).

The fighters make us welcome. They are obviously very young, and their weapons consist basically of Kalashnikovs and rocket-launchers. They insist that we visit their little shelter, which was badly hit the night before. They point out two patches of blood on the stairs going down. Here they lost one of their comrades, at four o'clock this morning. What happened? 'Helicopters came over and lowered two tanks onto the hillside. As soon as they touched the ground, they started firing at us. We took cover in this shelter, which faces the sea. Then we went to the top of the stairs, and we fired some B7 rockets at them. That was when they got our friend. But their strategy didn't work. They were forced to go back to join the main body of their forces, and we're still holding our position.'

Nothing to offer – but gunfire

As we go further down the road, we come to a large Syrian radar installation on top of a hill. It has been there for a long time, and the people of Beirut know it well. The Amal militia inform us that it has been taken by the Israelis, and that they have set up heavy artillery by the side of it. Presumably the same artillery that will be shelling us in a minute.

Our two cars leave the frontline driving fast. We look back down the road. Once again shellfire is exploding on the ground, throwing up big white clouds of smoke. The Israelis are shelling not only the place that we have just left a few minutes earlier, but also the road we have just driven down. It's still a bit early for sighs of relief. At last we reach Beirut. It is 3.30 p.m. The least that can be said is that the ceasefire has not been respected, except by the Syrians. It is difficult to see what the Israelis have to offer either the Palestinians or their Lebanese allies, except bombing and shelling.

(Beirut, 11 June 1982)

11 June:

Ceasefire with Syria declared by unanimous Israeli cabinet vote. Israeli defence minister Sharon emphasises that this does not apply to Palestinians and that 'mopping-up operations' will continue against all Palestinian guerrillas remaining south of the line where the Israeli 3-pronged advance has halted.

12 June:

Israel continues to bomb Palestinian camps and the heart of West Beirut. Palestinian heat-seeking missiles fail to hit any planes.
— At Habib's insistence, Israel and the PLO agree to a ceasefire at 9 p.m.
— Palestine Red Crescent assesses Palestinian and Lebanese civilian casualties to date at 10,000. Of the city's 8 hospitals only one is still in operation.
— In Sidon the International Red Cross reports that its medical teams 'have used up everything', while '3,000 wounded wait for treatment'. (*Sunday Times*, 13 June)

13 June:

Sharon informs Knesset defence committee that 'the job is done'.
— In the evening the ceasefire breaks down, as fighting continues in Khalde near the airport; the road at Khalde is the last way left open to the mountains. The PLO therefore claims the Israelis broke the ceasefire 'so they could encircle and wipe out the Palestinian leadership'.
— Bombing of the al-Mazraa coast road and Sabra area continues with the Israeli jets flying lower than ever before, sometimes four at a time. The head of the International Red Cross committee in Lebanon, Francesco Noseda, says that more than 600,000 people have now been driven from their homes.

Sunday, 13 June 1982:
BEIRUT THIS WEEKEND –
33 HOURS OF PURE HELL

After a period of relative calm, today has seen fresh bombardments, first of Khalde, the areas surrounding the airport, and the mountains overlooking the road leading to the airport; then the heart of West Beirut. It appears that the Israelis are not happy with their present positions. They seem to be aiming to improve them – perhaps by taking Khalde, which continues to hold out, despite several days of intensive bombing – before calling a halt to hostilities. Journalists who set out this morning to take the southbound road, or the road to the airport had to turn round and come back. Although not as intense as Saturday, the shelling of the city's suburbs is still sufficiently fierce to obstruct movement.

The ceasefire negotiated by the Israelis on Friday (11 June) effectively put the Syrians out of the picture. Now the Palestinians are completely on their own, and in theory the Israelis could defeat them without too much problem. Midday Friday there was a halt in the shelling and bombing in the Bekaa valley and the centre of the country, but an intensification in West Beirut, the southern suburbs and Khalde. In the capital, the bombardments spread from the city outskirts and the Palestinian camps (Sabra, Chatila, Fakhani) to the residential areas (Mazraa, Basta, UNESCO). This is a response to the emptying of the camps: those Palestinian and progressive forces with arms are now scattered throughout the capital. The Israelis are also trying to hit the PLO leadership itself, which has now transferred to new, less exposed quarters.

At 7.00 p.m. on Friday the bombardments cease. But at 11.00 p.m. the noise of an approaching aircraft draws our attention. All of a sudden the night is lit up by a sinister white light. The aircraft drops parachute flares, which descend slowly, providing light for the artillery to start firing again. Sure enough, the shelling starts afresh. For kilometres around, buildings shake with the blast. Beirut shudders under the shelling. The next morning, the newspaper photographs show entire buildings reduced to heaps of rubble, or blocks of flats sliced in two, of sections of roof dangling like papier maché from their steel frames. How many victims? This will only be known once the sums have been done.

Looking down on the battle of Khalde

Between midday on Friday, when the Israelis negotiated their ceasefire with the Syrians, and the ceasefire negotiated with the Palestinians at 9.00 p.m. on Saturday, it has been 33 hours of pure hell, the worst that West Beirut and its southern suburbs have yet seen. Early on Saturday afternoon, a group of journalists decides to head up into the hills to get a better view of the fighting. From the roof of the University of Lebanon at Chouayfat there is a panoramic view of the scene. A 15-minute car ride towards the interior takes you to a village tucked away in the foothills of Mount Lebanon, overlooking the battle of Khalde. Stretching from right to left, with the sea behind it, lies Beirut city centre, then the southern suburbs, then the buildings and runways of the airport, and finally the beach which stretches to Ouzai and Khalde. From here you can survey the entire battlefield – or, to be more accurate, the Israelis' field of fire. We can see the mountains further south: here lie Keyfoun, Bchemoun and Souk al-Gharb, which have also been bombed.

It all begins with the sound of an aircraft. In vain, we scan the sky to see it. In order to locate it precisely, you have to pick out the areas where the anti-aircraft guns are sending up their little puffs of white smoke. There are far fewer of them than in preceding days. People say that this is because the Palestinians are saving ammunition, but the real reason is more likely to be the passivity of the Syrians. Since the previous day, by virtue of the noon ceasefire, the anti-aircraft guns of the Arab Deterrent Force (numerically greater than the other forces) have stopped firing. At any rate, with or without the Syrians, the anti-aircraft guns did not manage to shoot a single Israeli plane out of the skies over Beirut. The only visible effect of their efforts is to prevent the planes flying very low.

Here it comes. The plane dives at full speed, turns, veers off to one side, and drops its small round shiny objects. It turns and comes back again, dives over Khalde and levels out at about a thousand metres. Three small black objects emerge from the aircraft; they fall like stones, in a downward trajectory, taking a good two minutes to hit the ground. When they land, they send up a noiseless ball of red flame, a ball which is then surrounded by a cloud of smoke, which in turn turns into a thick mushroom. The transformation takes just a second or two – and then the explosion. The gap between seeing the light and hearing the sound of the bomb adds to the unreality of the whole spectacle, like a slow-motion film.

The sound of another plane approaches – or maybe it's the same plane back again. And, once again, the anti-aircraft guns go into action. The same scene is repeated, over and over. Five or six bombs explode at once, and the explosions merge into each other. The planes come back yet again. The little white puffs go up again. Once again, the bombs drop. The computers on board these F16 fighters are incredibly precise: despite the distance, the bombs always drop in the same place: the Khalde crossroads (the spot known as the 'Cocodi', where the Syrians apparently handed over their artillery to the Palestinians), the road to Janah and, further to the left, five or six positions up in the mountains. It's like a power-hammer repeatedly hitting the same nail. The regularity of the operation, its routine quality, and the fact that nobody seems to be able to stop it, are frightening.

The aircraft move off. A respite? Not at all. Suddenly there is a dull, distant thunder, like the noise of sheet metal being wrenched in two. It comes from over the horizon. Out there Israeli warships take up the attack. The ball of fire when the shells fall has a different shape, the smoke is not quite the same colour, but the net result is the same. The naval bombardment is no less murderous. And now the Israeli artillery also joins in. It fires up into the mountains, one shell every two or three seconds. By now the accumulated smoke forms a kind of continuous haze a good hundred metres wide, which covers the horizon. We see Beirut as through a light mist, in which fresh mushrooms are repeatedly popping up. A minute's silence. Then the planes start coming again. By now any inhabitants of West Beirut who have not managed to reach safer places must have gone to ground in their shelters. But what's the use of a shelter when you know that a well-directed shell might bring a whole building crashing down on your head? Khalde must be totally destroyed by now. What kind of miracle has enabled those forces still there to carry on fighting back? Because they *must* be fighting back – otherwise, why the continued bombing? Khalde is holding out. The airport buildings still look intact. The airport has not been hit. But what an onslaught, what an incredible imbalance of forces . . .

To get back to Beirut we have to take the road through Yarze, Baabda and Hazmiye, the seat of the recognised Lebanese authorities. This hill overlooking the city is the only place in the country where the Lebanese state exercises full authority. The rest is in the hands of the Israelis, the Syrians and the Phalange. Then we take a detour through East Beirut. The

Improvised swing, West Beirut

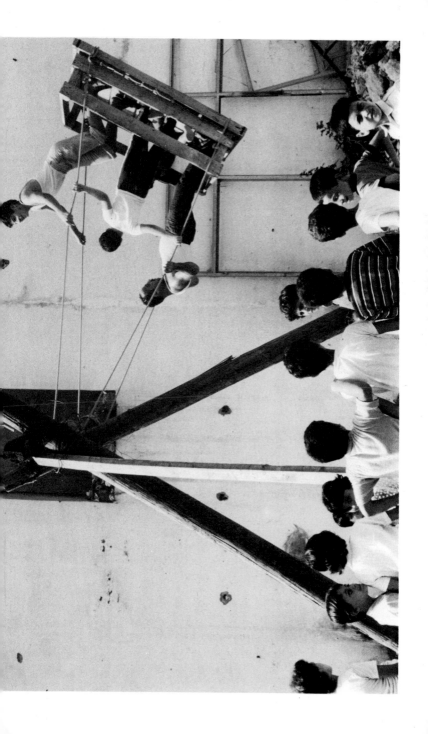

capital of the Christian part of the country is thriving: you can find petrol and bread; offices, schools, shops and even cafes are open. If this half of the city feels any compassion for the other half, it is hardly showing it. But at the same time, it is not gloating. Just a kind of tense indifference. You could almost believe that, here, everything was normal in the city – except that when you look up, you see the black cloud that hangs over the demarcation line between the two parts of the city.

We arrive at the Museum crossing point. The avenue leading into West Beirut is absolutely deserted. It leads into what seems like a ghost town. Only a few military vehicles are to be seen on the road, camouflaged with mud and driving up and down at breakneck speed. The only people in the streets are fighters. We reach the Syrian checkpoint. Damascus has left sufficient personnel in the city to enable the Syrians to claim, if necessary, that they have a presence in Beirut. The soldier waves us through. A little further on, the burnt-out wrecks of cars, rubble and broken glass are strewn across the road. Those Syrian soldiers were not there when we came through two hours previously.

The 33 hours of hell suffered by the capital and its suburbs since the first ceasefire came into effect appear to have been motivated by a psychological rather than a military intent. For this was not a series of bombing raids, but a punitive operation to demonstrate who is master. If, on Friday and Saturday, Beirut and Khalde were hammered by Israeli bombs, this is because the Israelis saw fit to sow terror far and wide before sitting down at the negotiating table.

Late afternoon: Israeli artillery has once again started to pound West Beirut with an intense bombardment.

(Beirut, 13 June 1982)

14 June:

Israeli troops complete their encirclement of Palestinians in West Beirut, claiming to have trapped between 5,000 and 7,000 guerrillas.

— The Soviet Union warns for the first time that the Israeli invasion directly affects her interests. The statement, carried by the Tass news agency, describes it as 'a criminal act of genocide' and elaborates: 'The Middle East is an area situated in the direct vicinity of the Soviet Union's southern borders and events there are bound to affect the interests of the USSR.'

— General Rafael Eitan, Israeli chief of staff, says that not all objectives have yet been completed. While Eitan claims that Yasser Arafat had taken refuge in a foreign embassy, Arafat tours Palestinian positions in the city, stating 'There is no power on earth which can make us lay down our arms.'

— Israel turns down two appeals for a ceasefire from the PLO delivered by the Egyptian ambassador in Tel Aviv.

— Sharon takes over Lebanese army barracks at Baabda and meets Maronite leaders in East Beirut.

— US government expresses approval of new 'coalition' Lebanese government.

Monday, 14 June 1982: VOYAGE ON THE FRONT LINE

You would think you were dreaming. Yes, it's Israelis that you're seeing, walking around, two kilometres from Beirut. Traffic conditions are normal on the road to Baabda. In the midst of the traffic jam that we are trying to get through, an armoured car overtakes with Israeli soldiers on board. People on the pavement wave to them, and they smile back. At first we had taken them for Lebanese army personnel: that would have been quite normal. The Hazmiyeh–Baabda–Yarze hill is the only spot actually under the authority of the legally constituted Lebanese government. But we were mistaken.

There was an even greater surprise waiting in Baabda's central square: tanks and troop transporters parked up the middle of the teeming square, under an ageing portrait of Camille Chamoun, one of the right-wing Christian leaders. The Israeli soldiers wore the word *Tsahal* (Israeli army) emblazoned on their uniforms. They were fraternising with militia wearing the words 'Lebanese Forces' (i.e. Phalangists) on theirs. They leaned on each others' shoulders; they slapped each other on the back. Women, girls and country people gathered in the square, and watched (sympathetically) the dust-covered conquerors. All around, the inhabitants of Baabda drank their coffee and smoked their *nargilehs* on their balconies. One tank driver ran a string round the turret of his tank and hung out a vest and a pair of socks to dry. Another lay in the cool in the shadow of his tank. The sun was beating down.

Outside the main post office in Baabda the various uniforms intermingled. I came across some Lebanese soldiers who, putting down their pistols and machine guns, had come closer to view this irresistible army.

Everything was so relaxed that the Israelis appeared to be taking no precautions. In the open entrance hall of the post office, an officer, his field cap jammed down over his eyes, spread out a map, marked out into distinct zones. It was in Hebrew. The junior officers crowded round, to get their instructions. The briefing lasted ten minutes. Over the shoulders of the participants, a Lebanese private, a Phalangist militiaman and myself gazed innocently.

It was all fairly incomprehensible. But an order had obviously been given. The drivers got back into their tanks, and the soldiers set down on the wall the small cans of beer they had bought from the corner shop. The engines of the armoured vehicles roared into life, and the tanks began to move, fouling the air. Some of the tanks stayed there; others cut across fields and disappeared; others took a minor road which led down to Khalde. These we followed, but they stopped a few hundred metres further on, parked in single file. We waited for a moment. Nothing happened.

We went on to the presidential palace, a few hundred metres further on. The first Lebanese army checkpoint let us pass, but the second one stopped us.

'We're journalists.'

'Precisely. Journalists are the last people we should let pass.'

'Well in that case, would it be possible for us to ask you some questions?'

The young subaltern looked irritated. However, he agreed.

'How is it that you're letting the Israelis pass without firing a shot?'

'We're hardly likely to try to stop them. They're very strong.'

'But they're virtually at the gates of the president's palace.'

He paled, and didn't know what to say.

'Listen, I know what vehicles I'm supposed to stop and which ones I'm supposed to let pass. To tell you the truth, that's just about all that I know . . .'

On our way out of the little town, we were stopped by a local inhabitant.

'Where are you going?'

'We're going straight on, to try and get back to Khalde.'

'I wouldn't advise it.'

'Why?'

'In a few hundred metres you'll run into the Syrians. They're surrounded. Maybe the Israelis are going to start shelling them again, like they did at four o'clock this morning. You might get a shell landing on you.'

We went ahead all the same. The road was suddenly deserted. At the fourth turning in the road we came across a small group of Syrians standing around a tank parked under the trees. The tank's gun-barrel pointed at the Israeli positions. The soldiers waved to us, and we joined them under the trees. There were five of them, armed with Kalashnikovs and rocket launchers. Their faces looked lost but determined. No sign of panic. We answered their questions. Yes, the Israelis were up the road; yes, the population of the Christian village was welcoming them as liberators.

'How can you expect us to defend this country if the inhabitants welcome their invaders with open arms?'

'In that case, what are you doing here?'

'We are defending our honour, the honour of the Syrian army.'

'But the Syrian army is no longer fighting.'

'Maybe not, but we, we are fighting.'

'Is it true that you are surrounded?'

'Not at all. We can reach Khalde within half an hour.'

'Aren't you scared of the Israelis?'

'You know, you only die once.'

We continued our journey along the front line that surrounded Beirut. Chouayfat. Up by the university of Lebanon, Syrian soldiers had replaced the militia of the Shiite Amal movement, whom we had met two days previously. But their packs were ready, and they announced that, once their officer arrived, they would be leaving. A little further on, we came on a road where there were half a dozen barricades, a hundred yards apart, set up by the Syrians; they were deserted. The zone had clearly been bombed. Bundles of clothes and suitcases were abandoned by the side of the road. Whoever had left this zone, whether soldiers or refugees, had obviously left in a hurry.

A little further on, we met a more sizeable contingent of armed men. They were spread out in ambush positions along the road. They too had a tank. We introduced ourselves. The Amal movement was in command, and with them were soldiers of Fatah and the Lebanese National Movement. We didn't even have time to ask our questions: they launched into a tirade against 'the corrupt Arab leaderships and the Lebanese army that lets its country be invaded without firing a shot, and the corrupt politicians who were cooking up compromises behind their backs, and Walid Jumblatt who had surrendered the Chouf'. What did they think of the resistance in Khalde? Their eyes lit up. They said: 'At least we saved face.' What about the Israelis? 'We are waiting for them. We'll sell our skins dearly.' Weren't they going to withdraw? 'To go where? To do what?' Their eyes sparkled. What about death? 'A bad moment, that passes.' Would they like to hear the one o'clock news? 'Not really . . . we haven't listened to the news for a long time. We're no longer interested in politics . . .'

By taking a series of side roads, we reached Beirut airport by an indirect approach. The airport was still held by Palestinian and progressive forces, even though the Phalangist radio had been announcing since midday that the Israelis now held it.

Khalde was also holding out, but one by one these positions were coming under the threat of the Israeli presence at Baabda. All the invading army needed to do was to take the Chiah road to get to the coast, with Khalde and the airport on one side and West Beirut on the other. It would then have been possible to surround the most militant elements of the Palestinian forces and the Lebanese National Movement within a few hours. However, they were not retreating yet.

We passed in front of the place called 'Cocodi', which I had seen pounded for hours on end. The 'Cocodi' sign was still intact. As for the buildings, they had not been completely reduced to heaps of rubble. We had to zigzag between the shell craters. It was here, and on the neighbouring Khalde road, that the shelling had been most intense. Down below, several dozen men were resting. They hadn't shaved for days, but their eyes were bright with tension. They were suspicious of us. We pulled out our press cards as we walked towards them, and made reassuring noises.

Then one of them, a giant of a man, exploded: 'Since you're journalists, write that we've been fighting back since the beginning, day and night. If they hadn't had their aircraft, we would have made mincemeat of them. Resist, or die, that's our only choice. The whole world has sold us out. The Arabs too have sold us out. Write it, tell them, so that they don't forget: "You are dust, and you shall return to dust".'

Returning to Beirut, we picked up a soldier hitchhiker. He sat in the back, his hands crossed on his Kalashnikov. We wanted to talk with him, but despite his efforts, his head kept slumping forward against the barrel of his gun. He was half dead with fatigue.

(Baabda, South-east Beirut, 14 June 1982)

Tuesday, 15 June 1982:
INSIDE BESIEGED BEIRUT

You have to address yourself to one of the two young people sitting in the hallway of the radio station, their noses buried in their notepads. Hardly even raising their heads, they quickly write down your name, and the names of the relevant towns and villages. One hour later, your turn comes, in amongst the endless list of names that the radio announcer reads out: 'Mr X of Beirut would like to reassure his parents living in Sidon. He is in good health. He is waiting to hear from them. Mr Y of Khalde would like to reassure his family, living in . . .' etc. 15 hours per day; 4,500 messages per day; 54,000 messages in all since the hostilities began. For the normal listener, it's just a long and tedious list. For a brother, a wife or a cousin who have been without news of you, it may be the end of their anguish.

Today some of the announcements are a little out of the ordinary. 'Mr Z, who came from Baalbek this morning, is unable to return because the Beirut–Damascus road is blocked. He would like to reassure his family . . .' That item of news was alternately given and then denied ten times in the course of the morning. Beirut under siege, Beirut at war is like that: a flurry of rumours, a mixture of true and false news. This Tuesday morning the news is that the Israelis have blocked the main eastbound highway at Jamhour. 'Even if it's true,' says the director of the radio station, determined not to give in to intimidation, 'what can they do? Invade the city? Begin himself has stated that he would not do that. Bomb us again? How long will world opinion allow this to continue?'

(Beirut, 15 June 1982)

17 June:

US officials warn the Lebanese government that the Israelis do not regard the Palestinian areas of Fakhani and Bourj al-Brajneh as part of West Beirut.
— Begin flies to New York. *The Times* says 'he is sure of a hero's welcome'.
— Robert Fisk publishes an interview with an Israeli soldier: 'Listen,' the Israeli said, 'I know you are tape recording this, but personally I would like to see them all dead. I would like to see all the Palestinians dead because they are a sickness wherever they go . . . and for us, I guess, I hope you understand this, the death of one Israeli soldier is more important than the death of even several hundred Palestinians.' (*The Times*, 17 June)

18 June:

First 48-hour truce negotiated by the US.
— *The Times* reports that for the third day running the International Red Cross has been unable to deliver emergency relief supplies to Beirut.

Left-wing militia in Hamra, West Beirut

Official Israeli losses up to 17 June: 214 dead, 1,114 wounded, 23 missing.

Estimated Palestinian and Lebanese losses: up to 14,000 dead, up to 20,000 wounded, up to 600,000 homeless. 6,000 men held as prisoners without prisoner of war status (Red Cross and Lebanese police quoted by *The Times*, 21 June).

20 June:

UNRWA is reported in the *Sunday Times* **to be making almost hourly appeals in Jerusalem to allow in personnel and supplies. Lorries ready loaded in Gaza, Jerusalem and Damascus could be on the road within minutes with food, medicines and blankets for the 110,000 it looks after in the south and a further 83,000 in Beirut.**
— Philip Habib reportedly attempting to persuade the PLO to lay down its arms and go for a political settlement.
— Begin in Washington.

Sunday, 20 June 1982: BACKS TO THE WALL – THE PALESTINIANS IN THEIR BEIRUT CAMPS

Estimated population of camps before invasion:	
Sabra	20,000
Chatila	20,000
Bourj al-Brajneh	30,000

'Leave? To go where?' The question keeps coming back, punctuating the story of his life's wanderings. The question always comes back without an answer, obsessively, as if in itself it explained his determination to stay put, 'at home', in his wretched hut in the Palestinian camp of Sabra. 'What are they calling us? The refugees? the *aidun* [the 'returners', i.e. those who are going to return to Palestine]?' The words jostle to get out, tripping each other up. He wants to speak, and the tension that has invaded his body for the last fortnight overwhelms him. When he tries to explain it in words, for the sake of the outside world, it explodes.

'What is it they call us?' he repeats, for the sake of the young fighter who is our guide through the maze of the Sabra camp. 'The revolutionaries . . .?'
'Yes, the revolutionaries. But above all, above all, the *samidun* [the

'resisters' or, more precisely, 'those who do not retreat']. Note that well. Write "the *samidun*". That's what we are. Leave? To go where?!'

Only to smell the scent of Palestine

Sabra, Chatila, Bourj al-Brajneh. The three Palestinian camps in Beirut have their backs to the wall. For several days, people tell us, they have been deserted. But that is only in a manner of speaking. They are deserted in comparison with their usual teeming bustle of life. But they are by no means deserted when you see fighters, standing in groups of four or five, every 30 or 40 metres, when you see soldiers laying mines and criss-crossing the road with trenches; or the military jeeps as they career down alleys that are only just wide enough to let them pass; or the women and children of these families who have decided that they have no choice but to resist – in other words, to stay.

Our friend, whom we have met by chance, invites us to sit down in the little yard in front of his house, around the tree which he tells us he planted himself. We sit in threadbare armchairs, surrounded by metal cans in which our host is growing plants. He is 52 years old, a refugee of 1948. He seems in a state of shock, as one who has witnessed disaster.

Without stopping, he goes on to tell us the story of his life. He was 18 when the state of Israel was set up. He spent a year in prison before being expelled. Jordan–Gaza, Gaza–Jordan. He met Georges Habash in 1954. He went on to join the Popular Front for the Liberation of Palestine (PFLP). In 1970 he was in Wahadate, the big Palestinian camp near Amman in Jordan. He took part in operations, including hijacking aircraft to 'Revolution Airport'. The King of Jordan unleased his repression. Black September. He came out alive. 'Leave? To go where?' Lebanon has been his last refuge, his last chance. He found himself in Sabra camp. 'On this spot that you see, there was nothing. No house, no tree, no yard. Well, I would give all this up and live in a tent. Not even in Palestine, but just on the other bank of the Jordan, just close enough to smell the scent of Palestine.' He adds that if he has to leave Lebanon, he will stand before God with his head held high. His words would be melodramatic if the situation were not what it is.

But how far will Begin go in Lebanon?

Israeli shelling has drawn a new frontier in West Beirut. The shells have fallen on the areas to the south of Corniche al-Mazraa (heavily populated outlying areas, and the Palestinian camps). The more northerly residential areas have been spared. At each stage of this war – which has been steadily reducing the non-occupied part of the country – the Lebanese have clutched at every possible 'lesser evil' – something to which Israeli propaganda itself has contributed. At first people believed that Begin would stop at the Zahrani River. Then at Damour. Then at Khalde. Then at Baabda.

Now people think that Begin's campaign will stop short of an attack on Beirut. This is what people want to believe, even though they know that a sizeable contingent of armed Palestinians is gathered in the northern area of West Beirut, that they are building trenches and that sandbag walls ten feet high are now barricading the narrow streets that lead down to the sea. Begin, if he wants to complete his business in Beirut, will have to go further than just laying siege to the Palestinian camps on the outskirts of the city.

'Now,' says our host, 'all we have left is to show them what the Palestinian people are made of . . .'

'Show them? We're not going to show them anything! We want to free our land!' His neighbour joined in without warning. A dozen people had gathered to listen to our conversation. 'Myself,' she said, 'I am from south Lebanon. I have nine children, and I would sacrifice them all if necessary. But I will never renounce an inch of our land, not even one olive tree. For me, there are no Shiites, or Sunnis, or Druzes or Christians; there are only Lebanese, Palestinians, "Children of Arabs" and a country that is occupied. We have to free it, and that's that. Look at my daughter here. She's eleven. Ask her what she's prepared for the Israelis . . .'

'I'll drop bottles on their heads'

The girl is shy because everyone turns and looks at her. She blushes and lowers her head, and doesn't want to speak. The mother insists. The little girl finally murmurs, 'I've prepared three crates of Pepsi-Cola bottles. I'll throw the empty bottles at them.'

'Let them come,' her mother takes up again. 'If they're men. Let them come into this camp. We'll know how to welcome them. Not like those Phalangist traitors!'

'Is it true that most people in the camp have left?'

'No, it isn't true. We've got enough fighters to defend us. The others have taken up positions in the residential areas, on the seafront.'

'So, you are not ready to lay down your weapons?'

'Lay down our guns?!' the Palestinian replies. 'We've taken 34 years to get these guns in our hands. We're not going to throw them away as easily as that.'

It was the same story half an hour later, with a group of Fatah fighters defending the camp. A dozen of them surrounded us in the garage that served them as an office. We arrived at dinner time. The men were standing around a table on which was placed an enormous pot of rice and another pot containing vegetables. They were taking turns to eat from the pots. The mother of one of them was in charge of the cooking.

'The road to revolution,' said one, 'is strewn with thorns, not with roses. Particularly with the "Arab brothers" that we have. Among those "friends" we should give special mention to the "Syrian brothers" who have run off like rabbits and have only been acting on their own interests . . .'

'If the *Tsahal* want to attack the camps, they are welcome . . .'

At the mention of the Syrians, everyone adds their own bit. 'They say that they are part of the "steadfastness" front. What steadfastness is that? Myself, before this war, if I wanted to come up to Beirut from south Lebanon, I had to bury my rifle at Zahrai. Every Syrian checkpoint on the way stopped and searched me. Why? I'm not in Lebanon as a tourist, but to carry a gun. And the Syrian who stops me carrying my gun runs away from the Israelis, and lets the Israeli besiege me in Beirut. And Chouf mountain [a fiefdom of the Druzes under Walid Jumblatt] betrays us. But it doesn't matter. The cat, when it's surrounded, becomes a tiger.'

The men move aside to let through a child in uniform. They push him towards us with pride: 'He's a *Chebl* [a Lion Cub of the Revolution].' He claims to be 14, but looks no older than ten. The fighters say that he is the future, and that he will not retreat. With the same pride they introduce us to a fighter who is 67, an old man with a proud moustache. Are they up to date with the negotiations being conducted by their leaders? 'Yes. We have to negotiate, but only with respect for our rights.' Are they ready to lay down their arms? Out of the question. If we wanted to betray our cause, we would have fallen in with Sadat a long time ago.' Aren't they scared of the Israelis? 'No. In their leaflets they tell us to "stop and think", so as to get us to surrender. Think about what? We thought before we took up arms in the first place. Today, all that thinking is behind us.'

'It's going to be bloody'
They do their best to appear more confident and determined than they really are. To one side, one fighter says to another in an undertone, 'It's going to be bloody.' The waverers, the undetermined ones, have already left. It will be hard to get those who remain to lay down their arms. Later on in the day, a Palestinian officer confirms to us that the PLO has implicitly agreed to the Lebanese army coming into West Beirut. 'It's not a question of disarming,' he says. 'They're under an illusion if they imagine that we're going to surrender and evacuate the city waving white flags. But we are not opposed to gathering in weapons.'

These concessions will certainly not be enough to satisfy the Israeli generals who have pitched camp at the gates of Beirut and know that the Palestinian leadership is within their grasp. On the other hand, the leaders of the 'Rejection Front' (PFLP, PDFLP, pro-Syrian or pro-Iraqi organisations) are not showing the same moderation as Yasser Arafat. The military reverses have not been sufficient to bring about an unconditional surrender of the Palestinians. Even a surrender dressed up as an 'honourable agreement' will not be easy to impose on the defenders of Sabra, Chatila and Bourj al-Brajneh and the fighters who have dug in along Beirut's residential areas and seafront. In the car that takes us out of the camps, our Palestinian guide, who has not been very talkative till now, confides in us: 'Abu Ammar [Arafat] visited the front line today. He told us not to believe all the rumours of disarming and capitulation that we are going to hear in the coming days. He told us to hold firm, and said that the revolution goes on . . .'

(Sabra, 20 June 1982)

Monday, 21 June 1982: CROSS-SECTION OF THE WAR – FIVE STORIES OF A BEIRUT APARTMENT BLOCK

Religions of Lebanon

Christian Maronites: living in Beirut and the mountains of the north. A uniate sect of the Roman church named after the fourth-century St Maron, a member of the Syrian church.

Sunni Muslims: living predominantly along the coast and the mountains around Baalbek. Sunni Muslims believe that there is a chain of revelation from Adam through Abraham, Moses, Jesus (and others) to Mohammed and that each divinely inspired prophet reveals more of the word of Allah than his predecessor. Many urban traders, large landowners, and some Kurds are Sunni.

Shiite Muslims: living mostly in the northern Bekaa and the south. The 'protestants' of Islam who follow the teachings of Ali, the prophet Mohammed's son-in-law, and accept the leadership of imams (roughly equivalent to the ayatollahs in Iran).

Islamic Druzes: in Beirut and the central mountains. Most secretive of the sects, they follow the teaching of the prophet Maarouf, and await the reincarnation of the prophet al-Hakim. Until he returns nothing can be revealed and the faithful are divided into 'those who know' and 'those who do not know'. The Jumblatts 'modernised' the Druze faith and it is now a curious compound of Hindu, neo-Platonic and socialist ideas.

Also **Greek Orthodox; Greek Catholics; Armenian Orthodox; Armenian Catholics; Protestants; Syrian Catholics; Syrian Orthodox.**

In the official Lebanese Constitution, the president is a Maronite Christian, the prime minister a Sunni Muslim, and the president of the chamber of deputies a Shiite Muslim.

In the Mousseitbe quarter of West Beirut stands an apartment block. It is a microcosm of life in Lebanon. All the doors are open. Up the stairwell drift the smells of different kinds of cooking. On the first floor you find Maronite Christians; on the second, orthodox Christians; on the third, Shiite Muslims; on the fourth, Druzes; and on the fifth, Syrians.

Woman collecting water in Fakhani, West Beirut

You would have to see Madame Miza to understand. She welcomes us as if we were the sun shining into her flat, a welcome fit for princes. Yet it is the first time that she has met us. Her natural laughter, her way of telling jokes, her free and easy broadmindedness, and her large body at once put us at ease. A masseuse by profession, Madame Miza is a Maronite.

'With 40 children crying all around you, you only hear half the noise of the shells. So you're less frightened. Isn't that right, Nabil?'

Madame Miza's husband nods in agreement. He is a small man, with a slender moustache and a phlegmatic disposition. Madame Miza continues: 'Last night the shelling came pretty close. It was a real nuisance. We didn't get hit directly, but the house was shaking. I woke Nabil. I told him, "Nabil, the house is falling down." But we stayed in bed, in the dark, counting the number of seconds that separated the flash from the sound of the explosion. It helps you guess the distance, and to pass the time. Isn't that right, Nabil?'

She laughs again, and turns for confirmation to her children and the neighbours who dropped in when they saw us arrive. Mr Nabil goes out to make coffee. Madame Miza continues with the story of her war.

'On Friday the airplanes came knocking. Or was it Friday? I'm sorry – with this war one gets one's dates very mixed up. Wait, I shall ask my husband. Nabil! Were the airplanes working on Friday?'

Everyone roars with laughter.

'Anyway,' she continues, 'I tried to carry on working regardless. I went round to my clients, but most of them had gone. I saw my brother. I asked him: "What's going to happen?" He didn't know anything more than me. I said, "It's the same shit everywhere." I'm joking, but I came home with my knees knocking. I was really glad to be home – I said "*Alhamdulillah*" ["thank God"], as if the house was actually a safer place to be!'

With the Maronite Christians on the first floor
She came home with a supply of tranquillisers for the night. Yet to see her like this, lively and a bit capricious, you can hardly imagine her being afraid, or subject to insomnia.

She continues: 'The next day, they attacked Tyre and Sidon. Bombs started to rain on Beirut. All the neighbours came down into my flat. Everyone was chattering ten to the dozen. People were beginning to make each other nervous. One of my neighbours said, "That's enough talk of politics." Another replied, "So, what do you want to talk about?" The first one said, "We could play cards", but nobody really felt like it. Then one of them said, "Maybe they'll come via Christian territory, via the Chouf," and I said, "let them come and let's have done with it". We went down to the basement, because we felt safer there. It's stifling down there, but the noise isn't so loud. One neighbour was listening to the radio. He's a Shiite from south Lebanon. "They've taken the south," he began to shout. I thought I'd cheer him up. I said, "My poor friend – you had chickens . . . well, I'm sure they've eaten them by now. And right now they must be pulling up the onions and lettuces that you planted." '

Mr Nabil returns. The coffee is ready. But it's not a man's job to serve it.

Madame Miza runs to the kitchen, and returns to pass the tray around. She sits down again.

'On the fourth day, the area opposite us was bombarded, the area on the other side of Mazraa. We thought: "Beirut's turn has come." We began to think that maybe it was time for us to leave. But to go where? The convoy of cars that tried to cross the Syrian border and get to Homs was bombed. Fifty-seven dead. I'm sure you've heard. Those who took the Damascus road were pounded. When your time has come . . .'

The housekeeper chimes in with a quotation from the Koran: 'I do not run from my fate, for the sky is my sky and the earth is my earth.'

'Anyway, we calmed down and decided to stay. It's been worse than the 1975–76 war. At that time we were living in the area of the big hotels, and Phalangist shells were falling all around us. But that was child's play in comparison. At least you knew that the shelling was coming from the east, and that one street, or one block of flats, if it was facing north, would be safer than another, for example. But now, with the planes, the boats and the big artillery, it can come from anywhere. At that time, the shells would make a small hole and destroy one or two rooms. But now, if you're down in the basement, you're likely to get the whole block crashing down on top of you. Isn't that right, Nabil?'

'Absolutely,' replied her husband. 'That reminds me of a joke. Once upon a time there was a man who never understood why the village used to curse the memory of his late father. Every time his name was mentioned, somebody was sure to say, "May he never rest in peace . . ." Anyway, one day his mother confided in him, that it was because his father used to rob corpses. The son decided to act. The next time someone died in the village, he went and robbed the corpse of the deceased, and then stuck it up on a pole in the village square. The next day the villagers saw the body impaled in the main square. They said, "The father might have robbed corpses, but at least he didn't stick them on poles in the village square. May God love his soul. May he rest in peace." You see – this war that the Israelis have started will end by making us long for the good old days of the Phalangists!'

Everyone laughs, and the atmosphere becomes more relaxed, more lively. Everyone has their own little stories. 'Miza,' says one neighbour, 'tell us about your dream last night.'

'Myself, I always dream with my eyes open,' says Mr Nabil.

'He wakes up every time the bed creaks,' says Madame Miza.

We all laugh.

'The deep-freeze was full of meat', says the housekeeper. 'But with the electricity cut off, everything's gone rotten.'

'What about that dream, Madame Miza?'

'Well, I was in the flat. A woman dressed all in white appeared. She had a beard. I don't know why, but I was sure that she was the Virgin Mary, and that the beard represented Saint Charbel. She told me: "Miza, don't be afraid. Nothing is going to happen to Beirut".'

With the orthodox Christians on the second floor

On the next floor lives an orthodox Christian family: a mother with four daughters. The youngest is 17. She admits quite openly that she is 59 scared to death.

'I've had enough. I can't stay here any more. The first chance I get, I'm off! I'll go to live in Cyprus, or France, or anywhere. I can't take any more . . .'

One of her sisters reasons with her. She tells her that she'll never find another country like Lebanon, that she'll always be a foreigner wherever she goes. She herself is a secretary.

'Work is the first problem,' she says. 'I went in to work this morning. Obviously, there was nothing to do. But if you don't work, then you don't get paid. That's the way bosses are.'

Her mother, a French teacher in a private school, agrees: 'If I didn't have my private lessons, I'd never be able to manage. I'm talking about normal times. So, just imagine it *now* . . . We're five of us in the house, and there's the water, the electricity and the telephone bills to pay. Yesterday they were charging 2½ Lebanese pounds for a bag of bread [9 Lebanese pounds = £1 sterling]. Today it's gone up to 3 pounds. Aubergines are 7 pounds a kilo. Even the price of catfood has rocketed, and you can't even find any. We're having to feed the cats hamburgers. But they won't eat just anything. I've spoilt them . . .'

The family has two cats, one tortoise and three canaries.

'Five days ago we decided to leave for East Beirut. We took our Shiite neighbours with us. At the Phalangist barricade, just past the Museum, they told us that they were willing to let us through, but that our Shiite neighbours would have to turn back. I said that either we all went through, or nobody would go. They gave in. We found shelter with relatives living in Achrafie. It was unbearable. Even when you're staying with your brother, when you're not in your own home, you feel as if you're in the way. And anyway, all those Maronites look down on us because we're orthodox. They think that they're the only Christians. I wouldn't say that they're actually happy with what is happening to the Muslims here. But they're not exactly angry that the Israelis are breaking the morale of West Beirut. By the end of two days I couldn't stand the atmosphere any longer. I find that if I'm not sleeping in my own bed, I generally can't sleep a wink. Here, this is our neighbourhood, this is where we grew up. Our neighbours are closer to us than our relations. The war itself has bound us together. Here people understand each other. In East Beirut, it's all fanaticism. The Phalangists think that they represent the Christians, but in reality they represent only themselves. On our way back they stopped us at the same crossing: "Why are you going to the West? It's going to be terrible. Wait for a few days." I replied, "My dear sir, I want to go home. If we're going to die, I'd rather die at home." '

With the Shiites on the third floor

On the next floor, occupied by a Shiite family, the atmosphere is completely different. We are received by three sisters aged between 30 and 35. The eldest has shining eyes, and a perpetual smile hovering on her lips.

'I'll talk to you when it's all over. Today it's still too early.'

60 'How are you managing to get along?'

'We eat, we sleep, we read the newspapers, and we listen to the news, and that's it.'

'Don't you go down to the basement for shelter?'

'No. We're the only ones in the block to stay put.'

She's still smiling, but there's no happiness in her smile.

'I suppose you could say that we're used to it. We're from Nabatiyeh. In south Lebanon we're already familiar with the Israelis. But I'll talk to you when it's all over.'

'Why won't you say anything?' the youngest of the three interrupts. 'I've got a few things that I'd like to say. What do we want? First, the Israelis must leave our country; second, we want a strong and fair Lebanese government; third, we want the Lebanese army to face up to the enemy and not welcome them with open arms; fourth, we want the presidential palace to fire a symbolic shot against the aggressor . . .'

The third sister takes up the theme: 'If the Israelis enter Beirut, we won't be welcoming them like they did in Baabda, with showers of rice and carnations. We want an Arab Lebanon . . .'

'For my part,' says the eldest sister, 'I was happy when the Israelis arrived in Baabda and put their tanks in front of the president's door, and at the door of Victor Khoury [Lebanese army chief of staff]. Everyone could see the back of our beloved leaders . . .'

'The Arab countries,' continues the youngest, 'are nothing but traitors. South Lebanon was the only one to fight. The Chouf? . . . I don't know. I believe that the Druze leadership put pressure on Walid Jumblatt.'

'As regards fighting back,' says the eldest, 'we are fighting back. The only hard thing is that we've got relations in the territories occupied by Israel, and we still don't have any news of them.'

'And what's going to happen now?'

'There will be more fighting before peace comes. The end may be decided by a battle in the city. You only need to walk through the city to see it: there's no question of us surrendering . . .'

With the Sunnis on the fourth floor

On the fourth floor a whole gathering of neighbours is waiting for us. The men launch into broad political analyses, and the women tell us of their daily life. They tell us that we'd best not interview the Syrian family on the fifth floor. Given their situation, they would be hesitant to speak to us.

'This is not a normal war,' says the master of the house, a Sunni Muslim. 'This is a war of genocide. Now we're caught up in it too. The silent majority is now being hit, as well as the vocal minority. This is what the Arab nations want. In their heart of hearts, they would be quite glad to get rid of the Palestinians. This is wholesale treachery. All this began with the Israeli–Egyptian agreement [Camp David]. And now we are paying the price. At least Sadat was an honest traitor, though. In the end we'll regret ever being born Arabs.'

'The Lebanese state is going to be destroyed, with the active or passive compliance of everyone concerned,' his Druze neighbour predicts gloomily. 'The Lebanese has become a refugee in his own country. The whole world's solemn declarations will not console one single Lebanese child. I was in the Chouf when the Israelis came in. The Syrians fled from Jezzine to Mdeirej, a distance of 60 kilometres. The Chouf was counting on them. But they left their positions, one after another, and fled, along with the refugees.'

A third neighbour chimes in: 'It's not the Israelis who have attacked us, but the notorious American Rapid Intervention Force. They're trying out their weapons, sharpening their teeth. Take note: we would like to thank President Reagan for the presents he has been showering on Beirut.'

The lady of the house interrupts: 'We never expected that our "Arab brothers" would sell out two entire nations. The Palestinians had neither land nor sky. They were living on the sand. And now they're being chased out. They want to disperse them yet again . . .'

A fortnight earlier, Beirut had had enough of the Palestinians. Maybe the lady only believes half of what she is saying. Maybe she just says these things because we're the foreign press. But for the moment it seems that the bombs have given the inhabitants of the city a sense of shared destiny.

'All these children who have been killed,' she continues, 'what have they done to deserve this? What are we going to tell our children? And what will they say to theirs? What's going to become of my daughter? Even now, every time she hears an ambulance siren, she presses her hands to her ears and goes white as a sheet. Of course, we can rebuild the houses. But who can bring back people's husbands, their parents, their children, their wives? Who is going to pay that cost? It's a cost that can't be counted in money. And once honour is lost, it never comes back.'

(Beirut, 21 June 1982)

On the third floor of Gaza Hospital, Sabra-Chatila

Wednesday, 23 June 1982:
BUT THEN . . .

It's true, they've invaded Lebanon.
But then, they'll stop at the Zahrani river.
It's true, they've gone beyond the Zahrani river,
But then, they'll stop at Damour.
It's true, they've taken the Chouf,
But then, they won't come near Beirut.
It's true, they're encircling Beirut,
But then, it's only so as to restore Lebanese sovereignty.
It's true, they're camped at the doors of the president's palace,
But then, they wouldn't actually enter the capital.
It's true that they're bombing the capital,
But then, they're sparing the northern parts.
It's true, they've tightened their grip,
But then, the Americans are putting pressure on them.
It's true, the Americans are shutting up their embassy,
But then, the French are staying.
It's true, the southern suburbs have been occupied,
But then, the 36th ceasefire will hold.
It's true, the bombing is very heavy,
But then, it's a few streets away.
But then, it's the house over the road.
But then, it's only our dining room.
But then, my friend has only been wounded.
But then . . .

(Beirut, 23 June 1982)

21 June:

Henry Kissinger in the *Washington Post* describes the situation in Lebanon as offering 'extraordinary opportunities for a dynamic American diplomacy'.

23 June:

Zurich: president of Israeli Knesset claims that the amount of arms seized in south Lebanon 'would equip a million soldiers'.

24 June:

Copenhagen: Norwegian doctors claim to have seen corpses of 10 Palestinian prisoners in Sidon allegedly beaten to death by Israeli soldiers.

25 June:

US Secretary of State Alexander Haig resigns and is replaced by George Schultz.

26 June:

10,000 people demonstrate in Tel Aviv for immediate withdrawal from Lebanon.

Monday, 28 June 1982: NABIH BERRI – 'THERE IS A VICTOR AND A VANQUISHED'

> **Nabih Berri**, member of the Shiite Amal militia, is involved in the negotiations in Beirut. In the interview that follows he claims that a political solution to the war does exist, and that everyone here is more or less agreed on the scenario. The problem remains how to put it into effect.

We had to raise our hands over our heads before we were allowed to enter the apartment block near the Corniche al-Mazraa. The area has recently been very heavily bombarded. The flat is guarded by half a dozen armed men. On the second floor lives Nabih Berri, president of the Shiite Amal movement. He rejects the term 'Shiite'. For him, the Amal is a Lebanese movement and that's that.

Nevertheless it must be said that for the Shiite section of the population (reckoned at 43 per cent by Amal and not a well-loved section of the Lebanese community, always getting the worst of any deal) Amal is their sole political representation.

We are welcomed very warmly by Berri, a 40-year old lawyer from the south of the country, which today is under Israeli occupation. He is a man who does not mince words.

Nabih Berri: Now, there is a victor and a vanquished. We have to recognise the fact. We – in other words, the Palestinians, the Lebanese National Movement and the Amal – have lost the battle. It is to be expected that the victor will now impose his conditions. The Palestinians are going to have to understand this new reality. Today they are bound to accept any solution which does not lead to the definitive destruction of their movement.

Libération: In other words?

Nabih Berri: The phase of 'Palestinian guns in Lebanon' is now at an end. The Palestinians are going to have to adapt to this condition, as long as it does not involve them losing face. The problem is that Israel is trying to impose a humiliating surrender. But if the Israelis go on like this, they will begin to be seen in the wrong by the West and the United States. This will lead to the development of a spirit of vengeance throughout the region. The first to pay the price will be the Arab countries which are standing and watching us; then the world which is watching us – a world which wants to see an end of terrorism, but which has effectively sown the seeds of vengeance.

Libération: Do you think that it is possible to arrive at an 'honourable outcome' for the Palestinians?

Nabih Berri: This is precisely the question. Negotiations are continuing all the time. I am involved in them. Today, in particular, we are hoping to reach a solution that will save Beirut (West Beirut, but also East Beirut), will save Lebanon (the whole of Lebanon), and will permit an honourable outcome for the Palestinians. A possible scenario exists, and everybody is more or less in agreement. All that remains is to put it into effect.

Libération: How could this come about?

Nabih Berri: If the Palestinians accept a demilitarised buffer zone extending 40 kilometres from the Israeli border, and if an international force were sent in there, then what need would there be for weapons? None. The Palestinian cause is not finished, for all that. They are a people three million strong who must have a country. What is one going to do with them? Put them somewhere else? But where? Myself, as a Lebanese, and coming from the south, I am opposed to their settling here. The clashes between ourselves and the Palestinians before the invasion began bear witness to this. On the other hand, we have joined forces to fight against the Israelis. We cannot permit an army to invade our country without reacting.

Libération: What do you think of the progress of military operations?

Nabih Berri: The Israeli war is, above all else, an aerial war. The Arab countries have not yet learned this lesson. Also, I always knew that the US administration was dominated by Israel, but not to such an extent.

Libération: You were involved, together with other major representatives of Lebanon's political parties, in the Committee of National Salvation. Is this committee now definitively dead?

Nabih Berri: This committee fulfilled two distinct and vital functions. The first was to enable the Lebanese to get together. It achieved this purpose. Today, if I want to talk with Bashir Gemayel [head of the Phalange], I am able to phone him, and vice versa. Barriers have been lifted. Dialogue has been re-established. This is a good sign for the future. We shall be meeting again. We shall lay the basis for new agreements.

For me, this basis must involve an end to religious sectarianism in politics. At any event, it is no longer possible to ignore the Shiites, or to exclude them from the Lebanese political arena. We are part and parcel of the political destiny of this country. What I hope is that the Phalange party does not fight this war on the side of the Israelis, and that they don't try to draw political advantage from the situation. That would ruin everything. The Lebanese army will take over control of the country, and will disarm the militias, all the militias.

The second mission of the Committee of National Salvation was to act as go-between between Begin and Arafat. We kept this up for as long as we could.

Libération: Do you think that the Israelis will withdraw from Lebanon?

Nabih Berri: How could I expect the Palestinians to go back to their own country, if I myself am not able to go back to my own? I'm originally from the village of Tebnine. If the Israelis do not withdraw, they will end by creating new Palestinians . . .

The girl who had earlier brought us refreshments returned to describe her admiration for the resistance in the area of Nabatiyeh. 'Could you please mention the names of the villages that put up the strongest fight. They deserve it. Jibchitt, Harouf, Kfar, Tebnitne and Zifta. In the last village alone there were 12 suicide-operations, by people wearing belts of grenades. Our brothers, lying on the ground, were holding B7 rocket launchers against their stomachs, pointing upwards, and firing them at the Israeli helicopters when they came to drop tanks and equipment. But these rocket launchers have a ten-metre backblast. So . . .'

(Beirut, 28 June 1982)

These 'suicide missions' were carried out by the Amal militia who come from the Islamic Shiite communities of workers and peasants in Beirut and the south, traditionally the poorest in Lebanon. They gained in strength and Islamic fervour after the Iranian revolution. Their spiritual leaders are Ayatollah Khomeini and the Imam Moussa Sadr who disappeared in 1979, allegedly kidnapped by the Libyans. Before the invasion Amal's Islamic fundamentalism led to clashes with more secular Palestinian groups, but during the invasion by and large they fought side by side, though there were clashes in the south over PLO guns placed close to Shiite houses. By now they had been joined by the first of the Iranian volunteers, 500 of whom had taken up positions in the mountains outside Beirut at Souk al-Gharb, and with whom they share the 'glorification of martyrdom' that makes such suicide missions possible: some went into battle already dressed in shrouds.

The Palestinian fighters had a different technique for close-range launching of rockets against tanks. The aim was not to lose men. The Israelis called them 'ghost attacks' because they could not see the assailant. At night the fighter would stand in a hole in the ground, deep enough to duck down into, but shallow enough to give the rocket its backblast clearance space above ground. He would fire at a range of 25 metres then duck down beneath the surface of the earth, invisible. Such techniques were developed because with rocket launchers you only have one chance: the enemy can see clearly from the backblast where the rocket came from.

28 June:

President Mubarak of Egypt announces that he will provide a haven for 3,000 Palestinian guerrillas if the US commits itself to finding a homeland for them. He calls on the PLO to recognise Israel.

— President Reagan suspends indefinitely the delivery of cluster bombs to Israel. This is described as a policy decision and not a legal determination on whether Israel had been in violation of the bilateral agreements on the use of cluster bombs.

30 June:

Sharon announces to Knesset that Israeli objectives now extend beyond the 40km security zone. Now the government has decided 'the PLO must cease to exist'.

— Begin, speaking in Tel Aviv, warns citizens of Beirut: 'Flee for your lives, by car or on foot. Leave West Beirut.'

Father comforting his son, Gaza Hospital

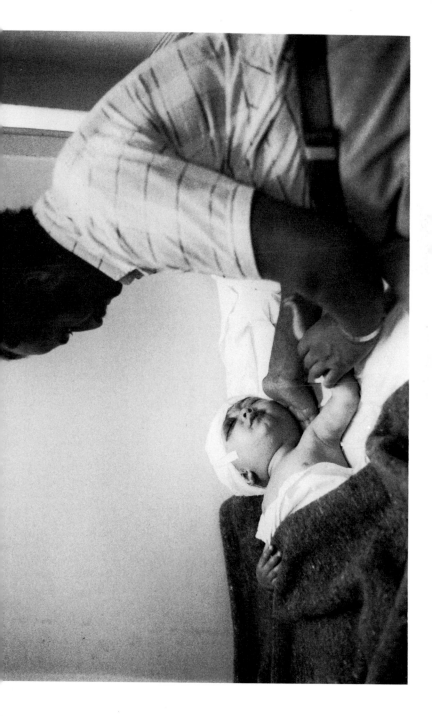

Thursday, 1 July 1982:
HOUEIDA DIA (AGED 12), VICTIM OF A FRAGMENTATION BOMB

She was helping her mother hang out the washing when she stepped on a round metal object the size of a melon. The pressure of her foot set off the detonator. The fragmentation bomb came out of the ground as it exploded, whizzing round and scattering fragments of shrapnel in all directions. The shrapnel from a normal shell kills only when it hits some vital part of the body – it may wound only a hand or a foot. You have a chance of escaping with your life. But there was no such chance for Houeida. She was 12 years old. Her name was Houeida Dia. She lived in Sfair, in the southern part of Beirut.

As our car stops outside the Acca Hospital, a young woman comes to meet us. She wears no nurses's uniform, but looks like a nurse. She speaks in a flat voice, her eyes betraying no emotion. It is she who tells us, without prompting, the story of Houeida, in all its details.

The registrar let us see the hospital admissions register. The following are the facts, as recorded by the hospital's doctors: on 17 June, Samir Ahmad Kurmo, aged 3, had his left hand burned by a phosphorous bomb that fell on Horch (South Beirut). He survived. The same day, a 9-year-old girl (only her first name is recorded – Suzanne) died on arrival at the Gaza Hospital (Palestinian hospitals are named after towns in Palestine). She died of widespread phosphorous burns. Then, on 24 June, in Bourj al-Brajneh, next to the Palace cinema, Ahmed Sakka, aged 32, was injured by an exploding phosphorous bomb. He died from his injuries. On 25 June, according to the same witnesses, Samir Kamel (22), Khalil El-Hajj (22), Said Ahmad (28) and Samir Khalil (27) died from burns. Once again, these were phosphorous burns. There is no record of any napalm burns. Phosphorous burns are recognisable by their colour – yellowish – and the swelling that surrounds the wound. No sign of shrapnel, and no pus. Immediate formation of dried blood, and a smell of matches.

Amal Chamaa, a young woman doctor in her early thirties, is in charge of emergency outpatients at the Barbir Hospital. She tells us that she has seen only one case of phosphorous burns. The shell fell on Bourj al-Brajneh on 14 June. The victim was Hassan Hodrouj, aged 40. Phosphorous burns, she tells us, are treated much the same as other burns: you wash them and cover them with an ointment that marks out the location of the phosphorous. It can then be removed, in order to prevent continued burning. However this treatment was not able to save Hodrouj.

The doctor also told us that a boy had been brought to the hospital with his stomach all swollen. The nurses and doctors who came into physical contact with him reported itching on their hands. They say this was not a case of 'nerve gas'. But on the other hand, there are rumours that nerve gas 70 was used in the capture of Beaufort Castle, the main stronghold of the

Palestinian forces in southern Lebanon.

In the heart of West Beirut, the Triumph Hotel (a hotel owned by Palestinians) has been transformed into a field hospital. Said Hegazi, aged 20, lies there. He looks extremely weak. Lying on his back, he can speak only with difficulty. His arms (from shoulders to fingertips), his head and his belly are swathed in bandages. He has a compress on his nose, and the burns on the face are covered with a yellow ointment. A fly keeps settling on his face; his friends sit there and wave it off. He tells us that he was walking down a street in Bourj al-Brajneh on Friday 25 June, when a phosphorous bomb exploded a few metres away from him. He doesn't remember much more. He realised that it was phosphorous because his skin swelled up, the wounds continued to burn, and he had not been hit by shrapnel.

The use of phosphorous bombs, and also of fragmentation bombs, is explicitly banned under the Geneva Convention. Presumably dropping 500-kilo 'straight' bombs on civilian targets is 'permitted'? But that's another matter. For the outside world, these revelations may cause a degree of horror or indignation. But for the besieged people of Beirut, they are a foretaste of what is perhaps still to come.

(Beirut, 1 July 1982)

Friday, 2 July 1982: SAEB SALAM – 'THE PALESTINIANS RECOGNISE THAT THEY MUST TRANSFORM THEMSELVES INTO A POLITICAL FORCE'

Saeb Salam was prime minister of Lebanon before the civil war and is still highly influential. He is the traditional leader of the Beirut Sunni community and was the first Lebanese Muslim leader to meet Pierre Gemayel, now leader of the Phalange Party, after the civil war during which he had been a staunch supporter of the Palestinians. He is also head of the Makassed Islamic Committee, the huge charity which runs schools and hospitals all over Lebanon.

Libération: Yasser Arafat told us two days ago that there is no question of the Palestinians either disarming or leaving Beirut. Now, though, you say that the Palestinians are prepared to leave the capital.

Saeb Salam: This is quite normal. Certain things can obviously not be said until negotiations have been concluded. There is a time and a place for saying these things . . .

Libération: What stage have negotiations reached at this moment?

Saeb Salam: One has to make a distinction between principles and the details of practice. The resistance leadership is ready to leave Lebanon. But the *details* are just as important as the question of principle. Who is to leave? How are they going to leave? For what destination? What will happen to the thousands of Palestinians living in Lebanon? Would the PLO feel able to leave in an atmosphere of humiliation? All these questions are linked. To the last one, I would answer in the negative. We, as Arabs, cannot accept that the Palestinians leave in humiliation. Because the leadership of the resistance here is reasonable; it is moderate, and it is not terrorist. If one seeks to humiliate them, then one will see the development of a truly terrorist leadership, an 'extreme extremism' which would harm the interests of the whole Arab world and would destroy peace. Furthermore, it is also in Lebanon's own interests that the Palestinians are not made to leave under a cloud of humiliation.

Libération: This is what the Israelis are trying to force on them . . .

Saeb Salam: Sharon is quite ready to annihilate both the Palestinians and Beirut itself. He is quite prepared, under the very noses of the 'free world', to attack a city – men and women, young and old alike. Who is responsible for this situation? The United States! They have given Israel their unconditional support – these same Israelis who use fragmentation bombs and phosphorous bombs. Nobody can actually believe that the real reason behind the invasion was the attack on the Israeli diplomat [in London]. The invasion had been planned for a long time previously, and the Americans knew it. [This is an amazing assertion from the lips of one such as Salam. He has several times been prime minister, and was involved in the civil war. Although a Muslim, he is generally seen as a 'friend of the West' and 'supporter of the free world'.]

Who can really believe in this 40-kilometre buffer zone that the Israelis want to establish on their border? The Israelis are in the Metn [Christian part of Lebanon]. This is a military occupation. Previously we had the Syrian army cutting the country in two. Today, Christians and Muslims are helping each other.

Libération: And yet there have been violent clashes in the mountains around Aley, between Phalangists and Druze militia from Jumblatt's party.

Saeb Salam: This is the result of what the Israelis have been doing. It represents a threat to the future of Lebanon. I would call on my Christian brothers not to fall into the trap. If the Israelis attack Beirut, it will be not only Beirut that is threatened, but the whole of Lebanon. Here in Beirut we have so many Christians living in our midst.

Libération: How do you see the role played by Saudi Arabia?

Saeb Salam: The Saudis have done as much as they could. Egypt has also done a good job. Out of all the Arab countries, these two have done the most.

Libération: What do you think of Bashir Gemayel's visit to Saudi Arabia?

[Sael Salam refers us to the statement that he made the day before, that it is not up to him to establish 'whether Mr Gemayel represents the whole Christian community or not'. He will not say more. However, he does appear to have reservations about the fact that this gesture by the Saudi royal household has tended to validate the Phalange leader as a major spokesperson.]

Libération: And how do you see the attitude of the outside world?

Saeb Salam: I have asked President Sarkis and the Mufti to make an appeal to the outside world. I have warned President Reagan that if the Israelis attack, the United States will be held responsible. The PLO has agreed to transform itself into a political force. But it must not be humiliated. If the majority of nations are still capable of showing humanity, then their leaders should at least be aware of their own interests. As for France, she has lost a lot of esteem in the Arab world in the course of this year. But she has regained a lot during the past three weeks. What we are asking from her is to put increased pressure on the United States.

(Beirut, 2 July 1982)

3 July:

An estimated 100,000 people demonstrate in Tel Aviv against the war, and demand the resignation of Sharon.
— Israel cuts off food and fuel to West Beirut.

4 July:

Israel cuts off water and electricity to West Beirut.
— Chafik Wazzan, outgoing Lebanese prime minister, threatens to break off all future mediation efforts between Palestinians and Americans if Israel does not end its blockade of food and fuel.

Monday, 5 July 1982:
WITH THE NASSERISTS IN WEST BEIRUT

The Morabitoun or independent Nasserists are about 4,000 strong. They are Lebanese Sunni Muslims, most of whom live in or around the Abu Chakr area of West Beirut near Sabra. They are a mixture of employees and workers, and their movement is partly financed by Libya and Syria. Their Abu Chakr area was the only part of West Beirut which the Israelis failed to enter. Their leader Brahim Kolleilat was alone in the Lebanese National Movement in opposing the evacuation of the PLO.

The Morabitoun (the independent Nasserists), one of the main organisations within the left-wing Lebanese National Movement, have their headquarters near the Abdul Nasser mosque, whose minaret is crowned with a large radio aerial. It is this aerial which transmits 'The Voice of Arab Lebanon'. The mosque has escaped damage during the shelling, unlike Abu Chakr Street, which runs alongside.

Along both sides of the street, every single house has suffered some form of damage, inflicted during the shelling ten days previously. The explosions were so powerful that the fronts of many of the buildings were totally demolished, leaving only their structural steelwork standing. It's as if the front half of the buildings had been sliced away with a knife, revealing each storey, with its broken lampshades, smashed furniture and shattered windows. Rubble covers just about everything in sight. Cars parked in the street were crushed by falling masonry. In the midst of the debris, soldiers of the Morabitoun militia sit in a circle chatting quietly. One of them shouts over to us something incomprehensible – but his V-for-victory sign needs no translation.

Inside the Morabitoun HQ the atmosphere is fairly relaxed, considering that we are less than a kilometre from the Museum crossing 'front line'. Trays of tea and coffee are passed around in the various offices, and the young women radio announcers give us a welcoming smile as they pass along the corridors. The entrance is guarded by sturdy young men armed with Kalashnikovs. They sit in a circle noisily cracking jokes. One of them is saying that before the Israelis arrive, they're all going to have to change their surnames, to avoid being recognised and picked up. He goes round the group, asking everyone what they would like to be called. Then he starts making puns on the names chosen by his friends.

Samir Sabbagh (number 2 in the Morabitoun hierarchy) passes by. We inform him that the Israelis are referring to West Beirut as the 'rat hole'. He answers, 'I would rather be a wild rat that fights its enemies, than a tame rat, a laboratory rat, like certain of our compatriots in East Beirut . . .'

A few moments later Brahim Kolleilat, leader of the Morabitoun, invites me into his office. He must be around 40 years old. He speaks a refined Arabic. The organisation which he represents is well implanted in the Sunni Muslim area of the capital. While other sections of the Lebanese National Movement (more or less influenced by the rapid exit of their 'Syrian allies') have tended to go into retreat, the Morabitoun continue to be a real fighting force.

Libération: By always emphasising the principal issue in this war – i.e. the Palestinians – people sometimes tend to forget its other aspect – the position of the Lebanese.

Brahim Kolleilat: Yes. We should make it clear to the world that the Lebanese National Movement did not arise out of the Palestinian cause. Since 1943, when Lebanon became independent, it has been fighting for its own political, economic and social interests. As Leban-

PLO fighter patrolling no man's land north of Israeli positions round Beirut airport

ese and as Arabs, we are allies of the Palestinian people who have been driven from their land. That said, we also have our own fight, for a true justice, and for a modern, developed country which will not be based on a 'pact' [the Lebanese state was built on a 'national pact' between the various religious communities]. The problems of our people, the suffering that they have to endure, cannot be resolved by a 'contract' signed in front of lawyers. We reject that. We want a country that is built on shared beliefs, on sovereignty and dignity.

Libération: How do you see the Palestinians' position since the start of this war?

Brahim Kolleilat: The Palestinian people are not in Lebanon of their own free will. If they were, they could just go home. They are fighting to defend their rights, and we support them in this. We are in favour of the Palestinians returning to Palestine, and we are opposed to them 'settling' in Lebanon. The 'other side' [the Phalange], by allying themselves with the Israelis, have succeeded in weakening the Palestinians, thus making such a 'settlement' more likely in the long run.

Libération: How would you weigh up the present military and political position?

Brahim Kolleilat: In our opinion, the Israeli invasion can be broken down into three stages: (1) up to the point 40 kilometres from their own border, the Israelis were fighting for their own interests; (2) when they went beyond Sidon, and reached the outskirts of Beirut, they were serving the interests of those international and Arabic powers who want to see the Syrians out of Lebanon; and (3) by moving into Baabda and then laying siege to the capital, they have been trying to establish a 'new order' in Lebanon, dominated by 'political Maronitism' [i.e. with the state under the control of the right-wing Christian Maronites].

Israel will make Mr Gemayel pay a heavy price for his alliance with them. The Israelis are as dangerous as the Syrians. They have a modern state capable of imposing a far more systematic domination on Lebanon's historically specific heritage.

Libération: How do you see the demonstrations organised by the 'Peace Now' movement in Israel?

Brahim Kolleilat: That demonstration is the proof that the Arab–Israeli struggle is not a religious sectarian struggle. It is also the blackest page in the history of the Arab world. That demonstration will return to haunt the Arab world like a nightmare. Jewish people in occupied Palestine have shown their solidarity with our movement, and at the same time, the Arab world stays silent. Imagine that . . !

(Beirut, 5 July 1982)

8 July:

Margaret Thatcher refuses to meet Faruk Kaddumi, head of the PLO's political department, on his visit to London, though the Foreign Office announces it is still studying Arafat's expression of willingness to make peace with Israel, as published in an interview with Israeli journalist Uri Avneri, 'to see if it warrants a change in the attitude of the British government'.
— Reagan states he will consider sending American troops to help with the evacuation of Palestinian guerrillas. Brezhnev warns the United States not to send troops in to the area. Arafat declines the suggestion that he should leave with the US Sixth Fleet, and warns that he and his *fedayeen* will leave only after US troops are deployed as a disengagement force in West Beirut.

10 July:

Renewed bombing of the Palestinian areas of Fakhani, Chatila, the sports stadium, and Bourj al-Brajneh. Syrian planes do not respond. Israelis shower Beirut with leaflets warning Syrians to leave.
— Greek government offers warships to evacuate Palestinian guerrillas.

11 July:

Ceasefire agreement achieved by Habib after heaviest day of shelling yet. Beirut police estimate 52 dead.
— PLO publish 11-point evacuation plan which includes deployment of French troops round West Beirut.
— Israeli invasion force now estimated at 100,000 men.

Sunday, 11 July 1982:
THE FOOTBALL MATCH THAT BROKE THE SILENCE

> **Football** Football fever was part of the legacy of the British Mandate and continued in the UNRWA schools with an hour's football a week. Before the PLO took over the running of the camps, 'sports clubs' were one of the few ways of being able to arrange inter-camp communication. Since the early 1970s the Palestinian national team has taken part in championships in Africa and Asia. Within the Palestinian youth welfare council there are sections for football, table tennis, boxing, karate and judo, painting and drawing.

A misplaced kick by Bossis. He blew it! How could he do this to us! Instead of the shout of triumph that the city has been preparing to greet France's victory over Germany, there are the confused grumbles and groans of a hope deceived. In the total silence of this dark night, people move around in illuminated apartments.

West Beirut is furious at being denied its happy ending. The match was 77 superb, admittedly; a game of clockwork precision. Everything was all set for glory. But in the end the baddies won and the goodies were defeated.

A misplaced kick! All through the two-hour match, there was no doubt whose side the people of West Beirut were on. If people support France, it's because they feel that somehow France is 'with us'. France's popularity is all the greater in that it was not assured in advance. Mitterrand's trip to Israel had even led to fears of the opposite. But today no capital city is closer to the hearts of the besieged Beirutis than Paris. So the least they can do is cheer their heads off for the exploits of the French team.

A misplaced kick! The disappointment runs deep. 'It's a bad omen,' someone says, only half jokingly. 'It'll be a blow to people's morale,' says another. 'But what a match,' his friend consoles him. In a way the sequence of penalties was a reproduction in miniature of the whole match. The French were not able to keep the advantage. And the Germans pipped them to the post.

A misplaced kick! For two hours people were able to escape from Beirut to the World Cup pitch in Madrid. They were in the comforting company of hundreds of thousands of TV viewers all over the world. The spectacle allowed the people of besieged Beirut to merge with the rest of the world's population. The enthusiasm that greeted the French goals was also a way of releasing a bit of the tension that has built up in people, however much they may deny it. The uncertainty of how the match would end, right up till the last moment, reflected, in a way, the uncertainty of the West Beirut situation itself. But the similarity ends there. The two rival teams – one with more heart, and the other with greater precision – were, leaving aside misplaced kicks, evenly matched. Whereas one could hardly compare the strength of the forces defending the city of Beirut with the strength of those surrounding it . . .

The match ends, and at once all the lights go out. Behind the drawn curtains people again light their candles and their camping-gas lamps. Once again Beirut looks like a city isolated from the world outside. Outside the shouting dies down. A gun starts firing again. One misplaced kick, and the fairy coach has turned back into a pumpkin.

(Beirut, 11 July 1982)

12 July:
After the bombing of three more hospitals: Barbir, Beirut and Makassed, there is increased criticism of PLO commando units for putting their guns so close to them.

Monday, 12 July 1982:
THE DESTRUCTION OF TYRE

Israeli figures for Lebanese casualties in Tyre: 56 dead. And the official Israeli version of sequence of events: on Sunday 6 June the Israeli airforce dropped leaflets on Tyre and Sidon warning the inhabitants to leave. There was a pause of two hours and then the bombardment began . . .

A young woman has managed to cross the lines into West Beirut. Her husband is with her. He is wanted by the Israelis. She experienced the fall of Tyre at first hand. Here is her story.

'On Friday 4 June there was shelling, but it only affected the Palestinian camp at Rachidiyeh and the outskirts of Tyre. Then, on the 6th, the shells started falling on the city itself. Aircraft, land artillery and the navy were all involved. The firing was so intense that we couldn't even make a run for the shelter – which was totally inadequate anyway. We stayed in the stairwell of the house. From what we could see, the bombing made no attempt to distinguish between Palestinians and Lebanese, civilians or soldiers. Its aim was to terrorise and destroy.

'On Sunday 6 June, at 10 a.m., helicopters dropped red, blue and green leaflets all over the city. They said, "Surrender! All the other cities have fallen." What could we do? We didn't even dare show our noses in the street.

'After half an hour the shelling started again. How can I describe it? It was even more terrible than before. The aircraft were firing special shells which are able to go through several layers of concrete before exploding. Some of them landed next to our house. Imagine – I had been so happy when we found a flat overlooking the sea! By now we couldn't even see each other because of the smoke which was filling the stairwell. All you could hear was shouting and screaming.

'We went down an alley leading to the house next door. Luckily, broken water pipes had put out the fire in the passage, but the building itself was on fire. We were able to reach the shelter which the Palestinians had built in the city. We stayed there from 5 p.m. on Sunday until 11.30 a.m. on Monday. The soldiers occasionally came in to tell us what was going on above. A group of Saad Haddad's militia strayed into the positions held by the city's defenders. Thinking that he was among his own people, the leader of the group, a man called Abu Emile, who is very well known in Tyre, introduced himself. "Welcome, Abu Emile," said the *fedayeen*, and executed him and his men on the spot.

'Five tanks advanced to the edge of the city. But they were met with rocket fire, and one of them was hit. So they withdrew. Then the artillery started firing again.

'In the shelter there was a mother and her baby. She only had one feeding bottle, but she passed it round so that all the children could have some milk. 79

As for the adults, they had had nothing to eat or drink since the day before. Also, the shelling was getting more intense minute by minute. We thought we were done for. We said our farewells. Then at 11.30 the firing stopped. We learnt afterwards that the Red Cross and the town's Catholic bishop, had won permission for the civilians to be evacuated to avoid a massacre. We came out of our hole. A Red Cross car had been driving round town with loud speakers, asking all the inhabitants to go down to the Rest House Hotel on the beach. We went there. The soldiers stayed on in Tyre.'

15,000 people under the July sun

'The whole population of Tyre was gathered on the beach. Between 10,000 and 15,000 people, standing in the sun. A Red Cross representative came and told us that the Israelis were demanding that the men of the city should go over towards the Palestinian camp at Rachidiyeh, to provide a human shield for the Israeli tanks, which would follow them. The news provoked utter rage and anger. The women began crying and beating their faces and tearing their clothes. In the end the men decided not to go. They said, "If we're going to die, then let's die here."

'After this episode, the aerial bombing started again. It lasted for four hours, from 12.30 p.m. to 4.30 p.m. Those were the most terrible four hours of my life. The whole population of Tyre stood and watched, helpless, as their now empty city was burnt and destroyed. Later, someone said that the reason why the Israelis destroyed the city so thoroughly was because they wanted to make an example of it.

'All of a sudden the bombardment stopped. There were flames all over town – it's not a very big town. Total silence followed the hellish noise of the explosions. Then tanks flying the Israeli flag began to move in on the destroyed city. The city seemed completely dead. But the tanks had barely reached the first houses when a field gun of the Palestinian and progressive forces began firing at them. It was miraculous. On the beach, as one person, we began shouting, singing and dancing.'

If it wasn't for their aircraft the Israelis wouldn't have been able to do a thing

'The tanks immediately turned back. They were not even out of sight when the planes returned to the attack. Really, without their aircraft the Israelis would not have overcome our resistance. They bombed and shelled with impunity. The building from which the field gun had fired was reduced to a pile of rubble . . .

'Then the tanks came back again. They advanced, firing cannons and heavy machine guns, and taking up the whole width of the road. Where they found cars in the road, they drove over them and squashed them as flat as a pancake. Once they entered the town, we didn't see them again. But we could still hear the Kalashnikov fire, and the sound of B7 rocket launchers.

'At 10.30 p.m. the Red Cross came to tell us that those who wanted could,

Exodus from West Beirut: Lebanese civilians take the Museum crossing to East Beirut

at their own risk, spend the night with them, on condition that they returned to the beach by 5.30 the following morning. Many people decided not to budge. The Red Cross had asked the Israelis (in vain) to be allowed to bring milk for the children, and to evacuate the seriously wounded.

'I saw doctors crying in helpless rage, faced with wounded people who were bleeding profusely, for whom they could do nothing. In the end a number of wounded were taken off to hospital – to an Israeli hospital.

'There was one man with his guts exposed. He was shouting, "I'm going to die . . . but please, not in Israel." They took him away anyway, and he must have died there.

'That night six women went into labour on the beach. Three of them were only seven months pregnant. The inhabitants of the town took it in turns to come and give blood. All the babies survived.

'On Tuesday at 5.30 a.m. the air force started bombing the city again. By this time it was obvious that they were doing it out of spite, just for the sake of totally destroying Tyre. Then they stopped. They went back into the city. Finally, at 4.30 p.m. we heard that the operation had ended.'

The menfolk are taken away. The Israelis look for informers
'The three Palestinian camps which surround Tyre were still holding out. We could clearly hear explosions and the rattle of machine guns and Kalashnikovs. Then the Israelis came and ordered all men between the ages of 16 and 60 to step aside from the crowds gathered on the beach. We all thought they were going to kill them. The women all began crying again, but what could they do?

'Later on, those who came back told us that they had been paraded under floodlights before being taken, one by one, in front of informers who were disguised behind hoods. Those who got through were given permits allowing them four days' freedom of movement. The others – most of whom had nothing to do with anything – were taken on a bus which left for an unknown destination. Now we understood why so many people had been taken in. Those who had done "nothing wrong" were told by the Israelis: "Very good. Now, we want you to tell us who in Tyre is involved with politics and terrorism." In this way, by a process of cross-checking, they were able to get a far more precise idea of the exact role played by those they had arrested. And at the same time they were able to break the morale of the "innocent".

'On Wednesday they began collecting up weapons. Some of these had been hidden, others left behind. When the Israelis found a Kalashnikov abandoned in the street, they would never pick it up themselves. They would get the children of Tyre to go and fetch it, in case it was booby-trapped.

'On Thursday food lorries arrived. We had no choice but to accept food from it. How could we do otherwise? I believe that the systematic destruction undertaken by the Israelis was intended, among other things, to make us dependent on them. With our economy destroyed and an entire population to feed, we would be forced to trade with Israel . . .

'Doctors were issued with travel permits valid for one week. One of them told me that an Israeli officer had said that they would soon be issuing permits valid for six months. Six months. Do you realise what that means? It means that the Israelis are here to stay . . .'

(Beirut, 12 July 1982)

13 July:

105 reserve soldiers and 17 reserve officers sign letter to Begin demanding to be excused from further duties in Lebanon.

— Dr Isaam Sartawi, member of the Palestine National Council and close adviser to Arafat, announces in Paris that the PLO has formally conceded to Israel 'in the most unequivocal manner the right to exist on a reciprocal basis . . . in sovereignty and within secure borders.'

— Saeb Salam, Beirut Sunni leader, meets Philip Habib in an attempt to arrange direct negotiations between US and PLO representatives. In Washington George Schultz says he is prepared to negotiate directly with the PLO.

14 July:

Lebanese government formulates demands for withdrawal of all foreign troops from Lebanon and a multinational army to evacuate the Palestinian guerrillas.

— Prince Saud al-Faisal, the Saudi Arabian foreign minister, has meeting with Reagan.

Wednesday, 14 July 1982: THE SIEGE OF BEIRUT – A SUNNI FAMILY

Beirut. Sandbags block off the ends of all the sideroads running into the Damascus road, which is now the front line. The fact that it's on the front line means that Ras al-Nabah is now an island of calm. You don't pass through it any more. You only go there if that's where you have to go.

Most of the shops, with the exception of the bakery, the chemist and the grocery shop, are closed. But the doors of many of the houses are left open to let in some fresh air. Here and there chairs have been put out on the pavement; people are taking the air. They will soon bring out their *nargilehs*.

For a moment you might almost imagine that the neighbourhood is so empty because everyone's on holiday. Those who are still here seem to be living life in slow motion. We run into the electrician. My friend, who comes from this neighbourhood, explains that, for 50 Lebanese pounds he will wire your electricity supply into the grid of the neighbouring streets. This will enable you to get twice as much electricity – in other words, when your street is cut off because of rationing, you can still run on electricity from other streets nearby.

Madame Hala K. is not very typical of the community she lives in. She would be the first to admit it. Coming from a Sunni family, she is, as she puts it, a 'convinced aetheist'. She raises her glass of beer in a toast: 'Here's to the resistance!' She is a small, smiling, attentive woman.

'Our neighbourhood is a mixture of Sunnis and Shiites. It contains some people who are very poor and some who are very rich. A fortnight ago, all the Shiites moved out – all of them. Newspaper vendors, dustmen, labourers, porters, domestics, etc. all loaded supplies into their cars and set off at 4 a.m. for occupied south Lebanon. Not a single one stayed behind. Partly they went to escape the bombardments, but partly they felt that their homeland in the south was slipping through their fingers. They preferred to be down there. In Ras al-Nabah the only people left were Sunni landlords and their Sunni tenants.'

She introduces me to her children – three girls and a boy. She also presents her husband, who comes in at that moment. She describes him as a *real* Sunni. What is a real Sunni? we ask.

'Those whose attitude to life is "This does not concern me." That's the way the Beirut Sunnis are. They keep themselves to themselves. It's because of this passivity that they have been pushed from second place to third place in our national political life. Once they were second only to the Maronites. But now the Shiites have pushed them into third place. It's just the same in our apartment block. I know my neighbours, but I didn't want to mix with them much. For a start, I don't believe in God – whereas they are believers, and fast during Ramadan. They have always looked on me as a bit of an outsider. My trouble is, I can't keep my opinions to myself. I say what I think. Anyway, my daughter told me that I shouldn't be so stand-offish. So I went to visit them. This was a fortnight ago. They were saying: "Beirut is going to be destroyed, and it's nothing to do with us. The Jews are coming to settle their accounts with the Palestinians. It doesn't involve us."

'Well, I couldn't contain myself. I told them that they were fooling themselves if they thought they could get out of it that easily. The Israelis were there, I said, to subject us – all of us, as Lebanese. And the Jews believe that they are the chosen people . . . You could have heard a pin drop. Then the lady of the house shouted at her children to go and play in their room, presumably so as not to hear such "heresies". My husband isn't like me in that respect. He doesn't like to be the odd one out.'

While she explains all this, her husband sits there without a word, with a slightly amused smile on his face. He reminds his wife that, unlike other Sunni husbands, he had let her go on a trip to the Soviet Union without him. 'Admittedly,' he adds, 'I changed my mind three times on the way to the airport, and turned the car round each time. Each time my wife said, "Please, the plane is about to leave." And I said, "Let it leave! How can you go and leave me on my own? I'm going to have to do the cooking, and look after the children? No way!" Anyway, in the end I took her to the airport. And two years later I let her go to the USA.'

Madame Hala confirms that this kind of behaviour is quite exceptional for a Sunni husband. She sighs: 'It has to be admitted that a Christian woman has a far more open social life, far freer. We Muslims are the victim of our traditions, and also of ignorance. People who read have more patience, a greater ability to get what they want. Myself, I am a primary school teacher, But what are my neighbours supposed to do with their time? They spend their time cooking. Ramadan, for example, is a period of "culinary creativity", a time for cooking elaborate dishes. So how do they find time to think about the political threat hanging over us? It's not only the Israelis who hold us subject. It's also the *hijab*, the scarf worn by Islamic women.'

Madame Hala continues thinking out loud. Maybe, though, people are changing anyway. Just before the blockade, one of her neighbours went to do her shopping in East Beirut. 'That experience made her begin to understand the real nature of this occupation. She speaks a kind of double language. On the one hand, she's worried, but on the other hand she hides her worry. For myself, I couldn't go to East Beirut any more. I find it too humiliating. Maybe she began to realise what it actually means when an Israeli soldier stops you, bang in the middle of Beirut, and searches your shopping bag . . .'

We sit down at the meal table. Madame Hala has prepared *mtabbal*, an aubergine purée, a potato stew, and some salad. She claims that it is nothing special, just what came to hand. We talk about the way the food blockade has sent the price of fruit and vegetables soaring.

After the meal, she takes up her story. 'Yesterday I visited my neighbours again. The atmosphere was not the same. They had read in the newspapers that the Israeli army is getting special warm clothing so that they can spend the winter in Lebanon. "That's news!" said the lady of the house. And one of our neighbours replied with a Lebanese proverb, which can be roughly translated as: "Before, the rain was gentle, but now it's pouring." They have begun to realise what's happening. I would say that the biggest disaster was when the Phalange allowed the Israelis to move into our country in the first place. You just don't open the door to a neighbour who is a hundred times stronger than you. They have destroyed our harvests and bombed our towns. Our service industries, our tourism, our finance and our agriculture, everything which made up the wealth of Lebanon, has been destroyed. To the benefit of the Israelis. This is no joke. Soon, even our sewing needles will be stamped with the Star of David. Maybe the tomatoes, the melons and the oranges that we eat today are already Israeli imports . . . The sick thing is that the Maronites are going to get more out of all this than the rest of us.'

(Beirut, 14 July 1982)

15 July:

Faruk Kaddumi, head of the PLO political committee, and two representatives of the Arab League hold talks with Mitterrand. This is the first time the French president has received a PLO leader, but Mitterrand emphasises this does not mean a shift in policy.

— With negotiations for evacuation at a deadlock, Sharon warns that time is running out for West Beirut.

16 July:

US State Department announces that 'finding a home for the PLO is an Arab problem.'

— Israel cuts off Red Cross distribution of essentials to displaced families in West Beirut.

— 'Major' Haddad claims that he has pushed north and now controls an area of 'several hundred square miles'. He discloses plans to increase his force from 2,000 to 50,000.

— PLO's offer to transfer their headquarters to Tripoli in north Lebanon rejected by President Sarkis during negotiations with Habib.

18 July:

At a rally in Tel Aviv an estimated 200,000 people demonstrate in support of Begin's policies. He tells them 'The murderers in Beirut do not have 30 days to leave.'

— US denies that it has withheld delivery of cluster bombs to Israel.

19 July:

Habib's 'final' proposals demand total withdrawal of Syrian forces and PLO guerrillas, and partial withdrawal of Israel to Sidon.

— First of the 12–16-year-old 'RPG kids' (Rocket-Propelled Grenades) arrested by the Israelis in June are handed over to the International Red Cross and put in special compound of Ansar prison camp.

20 July:

Drinking water, flour, fruit and vegetables allowed into besieged West Beirut, but not fuel.

Bomb scare, West Beirut

Monday, 19 July 1982:
ABU JIHAD, PLO MILITARY COMMANDER

Abu Jihad is officially the military vice-chairman of Fatah. Because Fatah is the largest group within the PLO he is often loosely referred to by journalists as the 'military head' of the PLO.

Abu Jihad himself opens the door to us, in a small flat 'somewhere in West Beirut', loaned by friends. The PLO's 'strong man' has a peaceful, fatherly look about him. Freshly shaved, with his thin moustache neatly trimmed, and wearing comfortable slippers, he hardly looks the image of the commander of the Palestinian armed forces – the position in which he stands in for Arafat. He wears a loose-fitting khaki uniform. No gun in sight. We are taken into a living room packed with books and knick-knacks. The only indication of our host's importance is the presence of a radio transceiver in one corner of the room.

Abu Jihad, real name Khalil Ibrahim Wazir, was born in Ramleh, Palestine, in 1935. He was one of Arafat's earliest friends in Kuwait, and was active with him in the formation of Fatah. From the beginning, his concern was with military matters. In 1963 he became head of Fatah's first office in an Arab country – in Algiers – and succeeded in opening a Palestinian training camp in Algeria. He was not even 30 when, in 1964, he accompanied Arafat on a visit to China.

In 1965 Fatah launched its first military operation. Abu Jihad moved from Algiers to Damascus, where he established his new headquarters. He was in charge of commando operations in the occupied territories. After the Arab defeat in the Six Day War (1967), Fatah took on increasing importance in the region. Abu Jihad commanded military operations against Israel from bases in Jordan, Syria and Lebanon. In 1968, Abu Jihad, along with other Fatah leaders, spent 45 days in Syrian prisons.

He played a crucial role in the battles between Palestinian *fedayeen* and the Jordanian army in 1970. With the defeat of the PLO, he was forced to withdraw to Damascus. In addition to his responsibilities as the military head of the Palestinians in the diaspora, he is also in charge of the 'occupied territories office', which organises the struggle within Israel itself.

He continued in these key positions through the civil war in Lebanon (1975–76), and then transferred his headquarters from Damascus to Mar Elias in the Bekaa valley. He was military commander in the battle of Bhamdun, between Palestinian and Syrian troops, in which the Syrian offensive was checked.

But the Cairo and Riyad summits imposed a compromise. The Syrian army occupied Lebanon, and the PLO leadership remained intact. This

compromise was disturbed by the Israeli invasion in June 1982.

As we settle down and introduce ourselves, the radio is still on. A news-caster announces that Begin is promising the forthcoming liquidation of the PLO leadership. Abu Jihad listens attentively, taking notes. Our interview is to last three hours. The first part deals with military questions, and the second with political questions.

Libération: How do you feel about Begin's promise that he will liquidate the PLO leadership 'in the near future'?

Abu Jihad: Throughout the past week we have been receiving news of these kinds of preparations: assassinations, 'special operations', booby-trapped cars, etc. If Begin thinks he can frighten us . . . We have always lived with danger. The list of Palestinian leaders killed by the Israelis is long: Kamal Nasser, Kamal Aduan, Abu Yussef al-Najjar, Mahmoud al-Hamchari, Kubeissi, Abu Hassan Salameh, Ghassan Kanafani, Abul Kheir, Abu Safua, Majed Abu Chrar, and others too . . . They have also attacked Palestinian leaders within the occu-pied territories: Bassam Chakaa, Karim Khalaf and Brahim al-Tawil, the mayors of Nablus, Ramallah and al-Bireh respectively. But they have not been able to silence them. . . . These plans are not new. Right since the early days of the invasion we've had to fend off assassination attempts, bombs dropped from aeroplanes, etc. If the enemy has to resort to such measures, it means that he is paralysed militarily. So we are expecting to see an increase in these kinds of operations in the days and weeks to come. We are taking all necessary precautions. We believe they will yet again fail. And even if they succeed in hitting one or several of us – it would be a delusion to believe that this will weaken the PLO revolution. The whole history of our movement has been marked by martyrs and sacrifices . . .

Libération: We have not yet had the Palestinian version of the military operations that accompanied the Israeli invasion . . .

Abu Jihad: We should begin by remembering that the enemy has the most powerful army in the region. It is stronger and better equipped than some European armies. Its firepower is greater than that of the armies involved in World War II. This, in principle, should enable them to advance at top speed, control the main roads of the invaded territory and achieve a rapid military occupation. Two weeks before the invasion, there were briefings between Israeli officers and Ameri-can strategists. The question which General Haig's men put to General Sharon's men was the following: 'How much time will you need to achieve a complete occupation of southern Lebanon?' The Americans insisted that the whole operation be completed in three days. Otherwise, they said, international, European and Arab pro-tests would put the United States in a bad light, which would force the US in turn to put pressure on the Israelis. The Israelis replied that the operation would take between three and five days. That was their estimate.

Thus the time factor was of prime importance. The Israeli army began to advance, destroying everything in its path. Nothing was 89 spared – civilians, farmland, animals, buildings, institutions, hospitals, embassies . . . a real scorched-earth policy in reverse.

Faced with such a deployment of force, our watchword was: 'It is no disgrace that the enemy tanks should advance; but it is shameful if they advance without paying the price.' So, our tactic was to establish 'key combat points', reinforced positions, which we held for long enough to delay the enemy's advance. There was heroic resistance outside Tyre. The enemy also had to pay a heavy price trying to reach Rachidiyeh, al-Bass and Ain al-Helwah camps. Dozens of armoured vehicles went up in flames. In one of these was the colonel who led the assaults on the town of Tyre. Beaufort Castle was one of our principal 'key combat points'. According to an Israeli newspaper, *Hamishmar*, quoting an Israeli officer who took part in that battle, the operation cost Israel 200 officers and elite soldiers.

It is true that we put up a fierce resistance, and that we caused them heavy losses. This was why, once they had destroyed the camps, they sent in bulldozers to raze them. They razed Ain al-Helwah, Rachidiyeh and al-Bass. Fourteen camps in all have been destroyed. Damour, where the survivors of Tal al-Zaatar had sought refuge, was crushed by heavy fire-power. The Palestinian colonel Abdallah Siam, who defended Damour and later met his death on the field of honour at Khalde, estimated that 3,000 tonnes of shells were fired into Damour. This was the Israelis' tactic: destroy everything before advancing. I must stress this point. Not one single house was left standing intact in Damour. Or rather, *one* was left – the house where the Israeli deputy chief of staff Adam had set up his outpost. In order to shelter from our shooting, he went, together with a number of other officers, down into the basement, where there were several of our fighters. They immediately opened fire . . .

Libération: Would you say that the Israeli invasion has not achieved its objectives?

Abu Jihad: Absolutely. It is quite clear that we succeeded in hindering their advance, which was our intention. They aimed to destroy the PLO militarily, in order to weaken it politically and strike a decisive blow against the morale of the Palestinian people. Once they arrived at the gates of Beirut, they expected us to surrender. They demanded that we hand over our weapons, and leave Beirut with our hands in the air, waving white flags, or Red Cross flags, or American flags, or French flags . . . But the facts bear witness. Past wars have accustomed the Israelis to rapid results. Today, Rabin himself has stated that the day of blitzkrieg warfare is past and gone. But despite the tremendous disparity of forces, a people's war has succeeded in blocking the enemy machine for long enough for international pressure to be mobilised. When the world shouted 'That's enough!' Sharon had still not achieved his aim. Even American society and Israeli society have been moved. And those who were preparing to send us condolences have had to postpone them . . .

Libération: And what about today? Beirut is still encircled, and it is still possible that the Israelis will launch an attack . . .

Abu Jihad: Yes. They have not been able to conclude their invasion with an attack on Beirut. So instead they have laid siege to the city and imposed a blockade, hoping that the Lebanese masses will rise against the Palestinian revolution and demand our departure from Beirut. Vain hopes. They may still attack. But Beirut is not Sidon. Beirut is not Tyre. Beirut is a forest of guns and reinforced concrete. We will fight them, not block by block, but metre by metre. Are the Israelis prepared to pay this cost, in men and material, to gain the city?

Yesterday the Begin government asked three generals to visit the front line in Beirut and give their opinions. The first one, Uzi Markis [who led the taking of the old city of Jerusalem in 1967], said that he would prefer a 'political solution' in order not to expose the soldiers to such great danger. The second, General Yeshiyahon Gavitch, a tank commander, said that the Palestinians were well dug in and organised, and admitted that any eventual attack would be very hard fought. The third general, Meir Amitt, who has held several posts [including director of Mossad, the Israeli secret service], commented that discussions about the eventual outcome of military operations were raising public emotions and that this was doing harm to the Israeli army and to Israel itself.

This said, they are now debating the two factors that are holding them back: the costs of such an operation, and its international repercussions. The last meeting of the Israeli cabinet was attended by the main military leadership: Eitan, Sharon, Saguy and Droro among others, with their maps under their arms. Presumably they have put the finishing touches to their plans for an attack . . . We are ready and waiting for them.

Libération: So far you have talked only of possible *military* outcomes to the war. What chance is there of a political resolution?

Abu Jihad: Right from the start of this war, Israel made it perfectly clear what she meant by a 'political solution': a total withdrawal by the Palestinian revolution, both its fighters and its leadership, not only from Beirut, but also from the whole of Lebanon. The Lebanese president, Elias Sarkis, and foreign minister Fuad Boutros, together with US envoy Habib, have shown themselves favourable to this demand. They have taken it on board unaltered. The result has been to legitimate the Israeli occupation, and to justify their blackmail of the PLO and the Lebanese national forces in Beirut. They were prepared to use any and every means – American ships, French ships, Greek ships – to get us out of Beirut and drive us out anywhere – so long as it's out.

But we have made it clear that we reject these conditions, and that we have a right to stay. People say that no country, Arab or otherwise, feels able to accept the Palestinian fighters. Well and good. In that case, they can just let us go back to our own country, Palestine. Our present situation goes right to the heart of the Palestinian problem. It explains why we have had to take up arms against our aggressors.

Libération: But you are not actually rejecting a political solution . . .   91

Abu Jihad: The Palestinian revolution rejects any political solution which does not guarantee them their right to bear arms. The gun is the symbol of our right to resist the Israeli occupation. When the people of Europe faced the invasion of Nazi Germany, they didn't throw down their weapons . . .

Libération: Yasser Arafat has signed a document which he has passed on to the Lebanese prime minister, saying that the PLO agrees . . .

Abu Jihad: The PLO has provided its answer to the national and Islamic forces in Lebanon and Beirut who were seeking an overall resolution of the situation in the capital. In the 11-point document presented to the prime minister and also to the French and Saudi authorities, we have demanded, in particular, the withdrawal of Israeli forces from the positions they have occupied around Beirut, and the intervention of an international force to guarantee the disengagement and ensure the protection and safety of those living in the Palestinian camps. You know the other points in the document.

Libération: One of the points refers to the Palestinian leadership leaving Beirut . . .

Abu Jihad: The Palestinian leadership has never considered Beirut as its official headquarters for all time. We have said that we are prepared to transfer our headquarters to some other place, as long as we have the necessary guarantees to continue discussions between our leadership and the other Arab parties concerned.

The problem is that these positions of the PLO, which are negotiable, have been rejected out of hand by the Israelis and the Americans. Habib rejects them on the grounds that Israel has rejected them. This obstinacy forces the Palestinian resistance to defend its present positions and to fight. We are thinking of the fate of Beirut and its inhabitants. We are doing our best to save it from destruction. But Israel's aggressive designs do not leave us much choice. We are preparing for a showdown. It was not the Palestinians who attacked – it was the Israelis. It was the Israelis who invaded Lebanon, encircled Beirut, and showed the world, by bombing civilian residential areas, what they are prepared to do . . .

Libération: Do you see any difference at all between the Israeli and US viewpoints?

Abu Jihad: Before this war started, there was an agreement between the Israelis and the US regarding the invasion, its strategy and its timing. In the course of its operation, the Israeli army went beyond the terms of the original plan, occupied a larger area than had been allowed for, and caused tens of thousands of dead and wounded and destruction on a massive scale. These excesses put the US administration in a delicate position, resulting in internal power struggles which resulted in the resignation of US secretary of state Haig. The United States did their sums again. They have shifted position, from a total support for the invasion, to a policy aimed at achieving the same ends, but

Fedayeen *on the front line near airport*

without incurring international disapproval.

Libération: What is your reaction to the statements by the new US secretary of state, Shultz, on the 'legitimate rights of the Palestinian people'?

Abu Jihad: The replacement of Haig by Shultz may have raised people's hopes. In fact, though, the change is only superficial. The US administration has not altered its position – namely that it denies the Palestinian people the right to build an independent state; it refuses to recognise, and rejects dialogue with, the PLO. Perhaps the condemnation of Israel's crimes by the press and American society have led to US to say a few nice words about our people. But, I repeat, the change is minimal. We do not expect anything from this administration. All they will do is continue the Camp David policies, policies which at best will grant a Palestinian 'autonomy' – policies which our people have rejected, and will continue to reject, both inside and outside the occupied territories.

Libération: So, the invasion of Lebanon has done nothing to alter your basic positions?

Abu Jihad: If they think that this battle can change the determination of our people . . . If they think that they can force us to bow before the 'pressure of events' and accept such policies, then they are under a delusion. Our people will fight back and will pursue their battle by all possible means until the United States recognises our right to live as human beings. We are not asking for the moon. Our only aspiration is the same as other people on this earth: to have a state of our own, a citizenship, a passport and a flag. Why must the Palestinians be the only nation to be scattered and oppressed, condemned to exile and the absence of freedom? Why must the Palestinians remain disinherited despite their bitter fight, which has lasted for decades, to win back their rights? Why should we bow before the American–Israeli conspiracy? [At this point my guide and go-between, who had enabled me to meet and interview the PLO's military head, puts a question:]

Question: Abu Jihad, if you had Begin and Sharon sitting in front of you, what would you say to them: [Abu Jihad frowns a little, and thinks for a moment before answering.]

Abu Jihad: I would say: trying to assassinate an entire nation is not the road to peace. I would say: the Nazis tried to exterminate the Jews, but they did not succeed. Despite the Nazis' crimes, despite the Warsaw ghetto, the Jews rose again . . . The Palestinian people has also risen again out of the debris, despite the policy of liquidation and genocide that is being used against them. I would tell them: we began this revolution in 1965 with a tiny number of fighters. This revolution has brought the Palestinian people out of their situation as refugees into a position as fighters, where they have won the respect of the world. I would tell them: even if you succeed in exterminating this PLO leadership – something which we intend to prevent – this will not bring you peace. The new generation will take up the struggle and will carry on the fight, because it is a just fight.

(Beirut, 19 July 1982)

22 July:

Diplomatic deadlock continues. Ceasefire crumbling as Israeli bombing raids and PLO attacks on Israeli troops continue.

23 July:

Renewed Israeli bombing of West Beirut followed two hours later by declaration of seventh unilateral ceasefire.

24 July:

Syrians shoot down an Israeli F4 Phantom bomber over Bekaa valley. Over next few days Soviet Union steps up arms to Syria.

25 July:

Yasser Arafat signs pledge to recognise Israel, accepting all United Nations resolutions, including 242. The 'McCloskey paper' is presented by six US congressmen: it seeks to pave the way for US recognition of the PLO. It is rejected by Israel and the US.
— An Israeli brigadier-commander, Colonel Eli Geva, resigns because of his opposition to 'Operation Peace in Galilee'.

26 July:

Renewed bombing and shelling from the sea in West Beirut.

27 July:

Habib in Jerusalem for 'last ditch' talks.
— Heavy raids destroy parts of the Fakhani quarter of Beirut, including the offices of Abu Jihad.

Thursday, 29 July 1982:
IN THE PALESTINIAN CAMPS THE DAY AFTER THE BOMBING

Chatila

The scene looks like something from the apocalypse. The woman, her head wrapped in a scarf, her baby in her arms and another child at her knee, is a living image of the tragedy of the Palestinians. When we mention this, she says: 'What tragedy?' shrugging her shoulders.

Then there's another problem – her smile. A completely devastating, radiant smile that lights up her face. The English photographer with me asks if I can get her to stop smiling. He wants a serious picture, a front page picture, against the background of a ruined Palestinian camp. But she refuses. 'Nothing will stop me smiling. As Abu Ammar [Arafat] says, "Mountain, this little gust of wind is not going to shift you". My house is destroyed? In that case, to hell with my house! I'm not going to get upset 95 over a little thing like that . . .'

She is very young. Behind her loom the burnt-out remains of what was previously the sports centre, bombed so many times previously, and bombed again last night. Yesterday you could still have driven your car into this corner of the camp. Today the road is blocked by two big shell-craters, three metres across. We have come into the camp on foot. All around us, the camp is in ruins. Of all the small one-storey houses that used to stand in the camp, only one is still intact.

A few soldiers and residents of the camp come and gather round us. Their suspicion of foreign journalists gradually lessens. We chat with them. Suddenly there is a whirring from the photographer's camera. He has succeeded in getting a serious photograph. For an instant, the very young woman facing us had stopped smiling. You can tell that she has something terrible on her mind.

'Do you see that piece of shrapnel?' she says, pointing to a piece of jagged metal, about 30 centimetres long, 'How I wish that it would fall on Reagan's head, or Begin's head, and split it in two.'

A journalist from *Newsweek* is with us. He asks: 'How old are you?'

'Any age you like.'

'Nineteen?'

'Nineteen.'

'You already have two children . . .'

'We Palestinian women marry young so that we can bring up new generations of fighters.'

Bourj al-Brajneh

The main street of this camp is buzzing with activity. The fruit and vegetable vendors have spread out their wares on the sidewalk. At the corner café a row of men sit, smoking *nargilehs*. You would never think that last night, and the night before, and the night before that, bombs and shells had been relentlessly pounding these streets. Viewed from the centre of Beirut the spectacle was truly terrifying. With each explosion the sky turned red. The clouds of smoke rising from the southern suburbs were so dense that they blocked out the moon and the moonlit mountains in the distance.

Yet today the passers-by in this street in Bourj al-Brajneh, a good half of them soldiers, seem completely relaxed. To understand, you have to leave the main street and go into the interior of the camp. The alleyways, the houses and the little pieces of wasteland are completely deserted: about 30,000 people used to live here. There can be hardly more than three or four thousand left. We pass down an alleyway running past an open sewer. The poverty of the place is striking. A few graffiti, a few badly fitting doors and, on the street corners, shell holes and the marks of exploding shrapnel. The vast majority of the inhabitants of Bourj al-Brajneh have left, seeking refuge in the centre of Beirut.

We come across a grocer who has stayed behind. He sits behind his jars of seeds and spices. His stall is tiny. He tells us his story. He tells how, in 1948, he left his native Galilee, chased out by the terror tactics of the Haganah and 96 the Stern Gang. He describes how Jews and Arabs lived together peacefully in Palestine, and how their troubles began with the arrival of the European Jews. He explains how he has lived in Bourj al-Brajneh for 34 years, and that three of his children live with him, while the other three are abroad – one in the United States, one in the Soviet Union, and the other in Yugoslavia.

'Why are you staying here? It's very dangerous.'

'Because we mustn't leave the *fedayeen* all on their own. Who's going to look after them?'

'What's your name?'

'My name is Palestine, and my mother's name is Jerusalem.'

'No, but seriously . . .'

'I don't want to tell you. I'm frightened that the Mossad [Israeli secret service] might do something to harm my children.'

As we expected, he stubbornly refuses to accept any payment for the drinks he has given us.

Mar Elias is the smallest camp with about 200 houses and 1,000 people, among whom, curiously enough, were some Palestinian Maronites – originally inhabitants of Haifa who fled in 1948. A further oddity was that women outnumbered men two-to-one there. Mar Elias was largely destroyed during the siege because it was one of the strategic sites of Palestinian anti-aircraft guns.

Mar Elias

Mar Elias is a small camp, situated to the south-west of Fakhani and near the Soviet embassy. We meet three armed men sitting by the side of the road. We ask them the same question that we have been asking people all morning. 'Where have the shells landed?'

They lead us into the maze of alleyways leading into the camp. The place is deserted. 'Three bombs fell here,' explains our guide, pointing to a mass of fallen debris. 'Several more fell at the other end of the camp. Last night we repelled an attempted landing at the Summerland beach, once the most fashionable beach in West Beirut.'

This claim is impossible to verify. We continue our tour of the empty narrow streets. A newly-built wall has collapsed; a new house bears the marks of an exploding bomb. But the bomb was not one of last night's.

'I must introduce you to the man who lives here. His house was hit a week ago, but he refuses to budge.'

We find ourselves sitting in the front room of a neat little house. Velvet-covered red armchairs stand against the walls. Our host is a 75-year-old man. He sits cross-legged on a mat and welcomes us effusively. Tea is soon served. We hardly have time to introduce ourselves before the three young men who have brought us to the old man's house all start talking, all at once. You can see that our presence gives them a chance to relieve the tension that has build up during the previous nights of bombing and shelling. They need to talk with us, and explain. They keep interrupting each other.

The old man starts: 'I am Lebanese, from southern Lebanon. I live here, 97 in Mar Elias, and nothing is going to shift me. Why do they say that Lebanon is divided by religion? I am a Shiite, and that lad facing you is a Maronite.'

'That's right. I am Lebanese and a Maronite, and I am in solidarity with the Palestinians. My name is Elias and I would not change it for all the gold in the world [to a less Arabic version]. This is . . .'

Our ageing host interrupts, pointing to our guide: 'And he, he is a Christian Palestinian.'

Our guide speaks: 'I'm from Bethlehem. I am a practising Christian. Look.'

He rolls up the sleeve of his combat jacket, and shows us a cross tattooed on his forearm. I manage to get a question in.

'You've got a bandaged foot. How were you wounded?'

'It happened last week, when the bomb fell here. I was on the second floor. It threw me down to the ground floor. I sprained my ankle. I was hit by a couple of pieces of shrapnel, too.'

He gets up, turns round, and shows us two holes in his trousers. 'Excuse my language . . . You've a young lady with you . . . Anyway, I got shrapnel in my bum, and it's still there.'

The assembled company roars with laughter. A sort of tense euphoria has filled the room. I say, 'You seem very happy, all of you.'

'Why shouldn't we be happy?' asks the Palestinian. 'We are alive, and we are free. We are not retreating before the enemy – we're holding them off. We've got something to be happy about. Have you heard what happened in Sidon? Have you heard the news about the Israeli colonel who resigned for reasons of conscientious objection? I repeat, why shouldn't we be happy? King Hussein may be king – but I feel more king than him!'

Everyone present agrees eagerly. A powerful sense of emotion unites those present. They seem closer to each other than the closest of families.

'And anyway,' continues the Palestinian, 'what can happen to us? We might die – but that would be good. Because from happiness to martyrdom, the road is short.'

At that moment a woman comes into the house. She is about 50, and has a 12-year-old girl with her. She is the lady of the house. She puts an enormous bunch of grapes in front of us.

'The grape vine was hit by a shell,' she explains. 'But it's still got fruit on it.'

'Why do they keep saying that Lebanon is divided by religion?' the old man continues, returning to his theme. Pierre and Bashir Gemayel say that they're more Lebanese than us! It's a lie. They come from Egypt, and they're Copts by descent. Myself, I can tell you the names of my father and grandfather and all my forefathers. Write it down. My father's name was Hassan; his father was Bakr; then came Ali, and Hussein. They are buried in Bint Jbeil [southern Lebanon]; Hussein's father was Ghassan, and his father Imad. They are buried at Jezzine . . . Would you like me to continue?'

'No, it's all right.'

As we leave, our host insists on giving us a present – a bottle of orange juice that he presents to the young girl accompanying us. It is impossible to refuse.

(Beirut, 29 July 1982)

30 July:
Seventh ceasefire breaks down after exchanges between PLO and Israelis and extensive bombings of refugee camps. Eighth ceasefire declared at 9 p.m.
— Eighteen Lebanese travel agents in Israel to discuss plans for future package tours.

31 July:
Phones cut in West Beirut.

1 August:
Heaviest bombardment yet from land, sea and air. *The Times* **estimates that 260 tonnes of bombs were dropped over Palestinian areas, including many phosphorous bombs – this causes a worldwide outcry.**

Sunday, 1 August 1982: WEST BEIRUT – 200 METRES OF HELL

For 13½ hours the people camping around the outskirts of Beirut have shown what they are capable of, without hesitation or moments of doubt. Two months ago, Ariel Sharon and Menachem Begin told the PLO to choose between surrender and death. Today they are still offering the same choice. As an extra bonus, they are punishing the city of Beirut for holding off Israeli forces for the past 57 days, despite the latter's superior strength.

5.15 p.m. yesterday: The ceasefire has been in effect for 15 minutes. Fakhani is no longer a Palestinian neighbourhood; it is not a neighbourhood at all. The ground has deep gashes in it; lumps of torn up tarmac mingle with loose stones, pieces of twisted metal, and crumpled pylons. A mattress has landed in the middle of what used to be a road. The two sides of the road are joined by a massive crater, 10 metres across and about five metres deep. We stop the car and proceed on foot. We watch carefully where we step: Israeli cluster bombs are the size of a lemon.

The seven- or eight-storey buildings at the side of the road are riddled with holes. You can see the sky through them. Flames lick at the edges of the gaping holes in the concrete. Columns of thick black smoke rise from a number of areas. The whole area is shrouded in a light fog, through which, in the distance, you can just make out the dark shape of the Arab university. A raging cyclone has just passed this way.

From out of this infernal landscape a number of human forms suddenly emerge, like ghosts, blinking into the fresh air. They are fighters, with their Kalashnikovs slung on their backs. They move forward as if in a slow-motion film, hardly able to believe the transformation in the surrounding landscape. They stop in the middle of the road, and turn to one another. '*Al hamdulillah a salameh.*' The ritual phrase. It is repeated by each of those present. They thank God, and congratulate themselves on still being alive. Already the shadow of a smile appears behind their dazed expressions. Nobody has been killed here . . . nobody even slightly wounded. Obviously, not everybody has been so lucky. In other places there were a lot of dead. But here, for the moment, people are hugging each other, happy to be alive. They shower the Israelis with insults and abuse. They still can't get over the barbarities that have been perpetrated. 'We're still here. What are they hoping to achieve?!' shouts one of the armed men, a man aged about 40, his eyes blazing with defiance.

We get down to exchanging news. The artillery duel was really terrible. The hellish howling din of the aircraft and the blast from their bombs are indelibly marked in people's hearts and still ring in their ears. The Israelis have indeed taken the airport. But it is not true that they have managed to cross the airport into the area known as 'Cocodi' (the name of the open-air café which used to be there), as Radio Beirut announced. Yes, it is true that a number of landing attempts by the Israelis at the Summerland beach have been repulsed. All this hellish bombardment of the southern suburbs of Beirut and half a dozen residential areas to achieve this paltry military result? Advance 200 metres and take the airport buildings and runways. To what end?

From a military point of view, this small advance threatens to catch Bourj al-Brajneh camp in a pincer movement, the other arm of the pincer being the positions between Hadath and Baabda which the Israelis have held for a month and a half now. But the glaring fact still is the huge disproportion between the overkill tactics – intensive and virtually non-stop bombardment sparing no sector of the besieged city – and the actual results achieved on the ground. Undoubtedly, if the Israelis decided to take the Palestinian camps – now 90 per cent deserted – then the taking of the airport would be a first step. But it is not possible that this was the only object of this sea, land and air bombardment, the likes of which Beirut has never before experienced.

There is only one possible explanation for this murderous onslaught – psychological warfare. For the first time since 13 June, the Israelis have advanced. They have broken with their war of positions. They have shown their determination to act. And that explains the bombardments.

They have also indicated, by using phosphorous bombs and fragmentation bombs, that they are not prepared to negotiate, even indirectly, over the evacuation of the Palestinians. What they want is for the Palestinians to leave at once, in single file, preferably waving little white flags. Without discussion, with no compensation beyond saving their skins. And there's more . . . General Sharon's forces are even refusing to draw back from the road earmarked for the Palestinian withdrawal – or if they do draw back, it will only be a few hundred metres. They want their adversaries – whose very existence they still refuse even to recognise – to run the gauntlet of victorious Israeli soldiers. Backed by their heavy artillery and their shelling, they can thus refuse Yasser Arafat the chance of saying, 'Our fight goes on'; so that he cannot raise his fingers in a symbolic V-for-victory sign. That is what they want.

The Fakhani neighbourhood is just one of the 55 sectors that have been ravaged by the Israelis' US-manufactured shells and bombs. But then again, the firing was not all one-way. While it was raining shells on West Beirut, the Katyusha and Grad missiles were firing on the eastern half of the capital, and the Christian-held mountain areas.

Corniche al-Mazraa was riddled with bomb and shell craters as I drove back into Beirut. The car had to zig-zag to get through the piles of debris and rubble. The area was unrecognisable. Smoke was rising on all sides.

At the moment of the ceasefire the main road was absolutely deserted. Forty minutes later it came back to life. Suddenly cars began to appear. Shopkeepers came out and swept out their doorways. A couple of street sellers set boxes of tins out on the pavement, a pack of candles, two cartons of cigarettes. And women, apparently oblivious of the danger just past, walked down the road, cans in hand, to collect water.

(Beirut, 1 August 1982)

Sunday, 1 August 1982:
THE PALESTINIAN CHOICE – A CAMP DAVID OR A MASSACRE

In the opinion of Walid Jumblatt, head of the Druze community and the Lebanese National Movement, the Arab nations may end up achieving little more for the Palestinians than what was already planned in the Camp David agreements. As for the future of the Lebanese state, he describes the threat posed by Gemayel's partitionist project.

The walls of the rambling family house are covered with portraits of his father, Kemal Jumblatt, who was assassinated in 1977, reputedly by the Syrian secret service. The pictures show him as a young man, an old man, in the company of various Arab and international dignitaries, wearing a Palestinian *kouffiyeh*, and, finally, on his death bed. The whole career of the former leader of the Lebanese left stands before me. And in the middle is another picture, twice as large as the others, a source of legitimation: the father, with his son by his side.

Walid Jumblatt welcomes me, wearing the outfit that has become his hallmark – blue jeans and a leather jacket. He is tall, and lean, with the look of a startled bird. His eyes express a permanent question. The bodyguard who showed me in now leaves. Coffee is served. Our interview slips easily between French and Arabic.

Walid Jumblatt is not a man given to ponderous formulas or the stiff, allusive, wooden language typical of so many Lebanese politicians. Five years ago, when he succeeded his father at the head of the Druze community and the National Movement, he had no particular qualifications for the post. He was under 30, and not at all interested in politics. But neither the Druzes nor the Lebanese left had anybody with sufficient charisma to take over from Kemal Jumblatt. So, both parties settled on the son who had the lineage, the name.

He survived the difficult period of Syrian trusteeship and the undeclared war. Then, on 6 June 1982, Israel invaded Lebanon. The first big surprise of the war came when the occupying army took the Chouf mountain, Jumblatt's fief.

At that time, virtually all the political forces in Lebanon seemed in agreement on the necessity of drawing up the terms of an 'honourable surrender' which they would then ask the Palestinians to sign. Jumblatt's attitude was crucial, given that the National Movement that he led was the PLO's principal ally in Lebanon. For a long time he refused to join the Committee of National Salvation, whose official function was precisely to bring this 'rule of the strongest' into effect as smoothly as possible. He finally gave way but then, following the terrible bombings of 24 and 25 June, he walked out of the committee, slamming the door behind him. This resulted in the break-up of the committee.

Jumblatt then decided to stay in Beirut, to share the fate of the besieged city. But there he felt cramped and confined. You would find him all over the city, holding discussions with journalists, ignoring the niceties of protocol, complaining sometimes of boredom, or perhaps of stomach ache, and handing out none-too-diplomatic judgements on the Syrians, the Palestinians and the Lebanese government. Behind his back, people complained that his positions showed no continuity, and that he was secretive and inclined to change his mind – a quality attributed to his Druze temperament. Several times when his hasty statements appeared in the press they produced mini-crises, resolved only with difficulty. But he carried on as before, apparently unwilling to change his ways. Last Friday, between two spates of bombing, he and some fishermen from his party took a boat out from the besieged city and went swimming.

Leaving aside these rather unusual goings-on, Jumblatt remains a key figure. As the head of the Druze community and the Progressive Socialist Party (PSP), he brings together Lebanese Islamism, the left-wing parties, and the Palestinians. Perhaps his apparent ingenuousness and the gangling stance are a defence against the pressures put on him by virtue of his position – a position which becomes increasingly important.

Libération: How do you see this unleashing of Israeli bombing over Beirut?
Walid Jumblatt: It's no longer 'Peace in Galilee' but 'Peace in Lebanon'. This means a lot of things. Israel wants to establish privileged relations – on her own terms – with Beirut. From the economic point of view, they want to destroy what is still standing. The proof of this is their continuous bombing, the way they have been pounding the capital. For one whole period, the bombing affected only the poor neighbourhoods. Now it's the turn of the rich parts of Beirut: the

hotels, the hospitals, the infrastructure of the city.

The food markets are flooded with Israeli produce. This is a serious problem for the farmers in the mountains – including the Christians – and in the Bekaa valley. As for industry, the bombardment of the industrial areas of Chouayfat and Naameh did tremendous damage. And don't forget Israeli designs on the waters of the Litani river. We'll have a heavy bill to pay.

The Americans and the Israelis don't want the PLO to evacuate Beirut. They want to annihilate the PLO by destroying Beirut . . .

Libération: Throughout this war, the Israelis have tried to separate the question of the Palestinians from that of Lebanon. They made out that if the Lebanese stood to one side, then nothing would happen to them . . .

Walid Jumblatt: But that kind of separation is impossible! The Muslim army in Lebanon is made up of Palestinians. The collusion with Bashir Gemayel and Saad Haddad indicate that Israel is getting directly involved in Lebanese politics. Israel wants Lebanon to have an anti-left, anti-liberal, anti-democratic policy to match their own interests. How can the Lebanese be expected to 'stand to one side'?

I would add that this policy also suits the interests of certain of the Arab countries, who see Lebanon as a hotbed of revolution. The Arab world is very conservative, to say the least. Its 'progressive' regimes can be just as conservative as the 'reactionary' ones.

Libération: At the start of the war, there seemed to be a certain wavering in the Lebanese position, in the position of your National Movement?

Walid Jumblatt: Yes, that's true. At one point we were completely lost. We did not expect such a rapid development of events, nor such a spread-out operation. The invasion was a shock.

Libération: And yet even before the invasion, some fairly precise information regarding Israeli intentions had reached your organisation and the other political forces in Lebanon.

Walid Jumblatt: We didn't take it sufficiently seriously. We expected an operation that would stop at the Litani river, at that famous 40-kilometre mark that was being talked about at the start.

Libération: How do you justify the fact that the Chouf was taken practically without resistance?

Walid Jumblatt: The Israeli army took less than three hours to get to Beit ed-Dine [in the Chouf]. This was completely unexpected. The Palestinian resistance abandoned their second line of defence at Rihane [in southern Lebanon] overlooking the town of Nabatiyeh. There were some pockets of resistance, such as Ain al-Helwah. But the military commander of Sidon, Hajj Ismail, lost his grip. The Chouf was only supposed to be the third line of defence. In conditions like these, I decided not to give battle because I judged that it would have been a useless sacrifice. I withdrew the PSP forces to the town of Aley.

Child torn apart by car bomb, West Beirut

Libération: How do you see the behaviour of the Syrians?

Walid Jumblatt: The Syrians fought a small battle at Jezzine, and then they withdrew. When the front line shifted to Aley, they realised that this could not go on. They had fought in very difficult conditions in Ain Zhalta, Man Souriyeh and Khalde. Their crack troops had held off Israeli tanks and planes with B7 rocket launchers. There were some bloody incidents. A troop commander in Chouayfat was forced to shoot 15 of his own men because they were seriously wounded and he couldn't transport them. I would say that the Syrians have done their duty by us. The problem is that there was no clear military strategy in the event of an invasion. In the Bekaa, the Israelis had a crushing military superiority in the air. But could Syria have done better than they did? Yes, I think so.

Libération: When the Israeli army found itself encircling Beirut, the question was posed of an 'honourable surrender' of the Palestinians. How do you now see the episode of the Committee of National Salvation?

Walid Jumblatt: I originally refused to join that committee because it was aimed against the Palestinians. Later on, the Lebanese thought that if I took part, I might have been able to save Beirut. It was stupid, but I accepted nonetheless. Nabih Berri [president of the Amal movement] had the same position as me. When it became clear that the committee was powerless to change the situation, I resigned. Anyway, things were no longer being decided here, in Lebanon. Were they being decided elsewhere? At any rate, Israel doesn't care what the world thinks. US envoy Habib has become Beirut's resident plumber and electrician.

Libération: At one point, all the Lebanese parties were virtually united in wanting to ask the Palestinians to leave . . .

Walid Jumblatt: Yes. I repeat, we were in a state of shock. Thanks to the Israelis, though, we picked ourselves up again. And today, what more could one ask of the Palestinians? They have agreed to evacuate their forces from Beirut, as long as they can save face. They have asked for guarantees for the safety of Palestinian refugees in Lebanon. That is hardly excessive. This is where the idea of the multinational force came from. President Sarkis and the Americans wanted the Lebanese army to undertake this task of separation and protection. But I insisted, and still insist, on a *multinational* intervention force. Its tasks must be clearly spelled out – to protect the camps in West Beirut from the army of Mr Gemayel Junior . . . But for the moment the main question is obtaining a ceasefire.

Libération: How do you assess the behaviour of the Palestinians?

Walid Jumblatt: They have done what they could. Abu Ammar [Arafat] has been adroit. He even went so far as an implicit recognition of Israel. One can hardly ask more of him in the present difficult circumstances.

Libération: Where do you stand as regards the Lebanese aspect of the situation?

Walid Jumblatt: We need a general disarmament and a re-establishment of legality. It's not easy. Each of the parties concerned in Lebanon will keep their arms until a general solution, a national agreement, is reached.

Libération: In your opinion, is such an agreement possible?

Walid Jumblatt: That's another question. We would need a new president of the republic, who would have to represent a compromise. Lebanon is a jigsaw puzzle that needs to be put together very carefully. The candidature of Bashir Gemayel does not represent a project for unification. This would be a partitionist project, a fascist project, and nothing more.

Libération: How does the National Movement come out of all this?

Walid Jumblatt: Some of the parties within the National Movement have chosen to go backwards. Some of them have become virtually Phalangist. None of them has escaped the shock waves. At this moment, the National Movement is slowly getting its breath back. But the old coalition has outlived its time. We are going to have to work out a new formula, more limited in its terms, less based on pan-Arabism, and more based on the social and domestic problems of Lebanon. All this depends on the answer to the question: what sort of Lebanon is going to emerge from this crisis? A unified Lebanon, or a divided Lebanon? If Bashir Gemayel manages to establish himself, then basic freedoms will be in the balance. We may have to think of going underground.

Libération: What is the situation in the occupied Chouf?

Walid Jumblatt: In the Chouf things are tense but peaceful. The tension comes from the Phalange militia that the Israelis have brought in. At Beit ed-Dine, for example, they moved Lebanese army soldiers out of their barracks in order to move in 150 Phalangists.

Libération: Do you see your political activity as continuing the politics of your father, Kemal Jumblatt?

Walid Jumblatt: At the Lebanese level, yes, since I reject the Maronites' plan for a Maronite hegemony, and I am fighting for a democratic and pluralist Lebanon. Today a reshuffling of the cards is under way.

At the Palestinian level, I would say 'more or less'.

Libération: Which means . . .

Walid Jumblatt: If the PLO were to leave Beirut in exchange for an agreement equivalent to Camp David, that would be a setback. Unfortunately, in the present conjuncture and the present balance of forces, I believe that the Arab countries will not be able to achieve anything more than Camp David for the Palestinians. There is a danger that the final choice will be between Camp David or a massacre.

Israel is not prepared to offer anything. The Peres-led Labour opposition has not even been able to denounce Begin's 'terrorist' occupation. If that is Israeli socialism, then the only hopeful political force in Israel is the 'Peace Now' movement.

Libération: How do you see the immediate future?

Walid Jumblatt: I don't see anything very positive. The destruction will continue unless a miracle solution can be found. The situation is rather gloomy . . .

(Beirut, 1 August 1982) 107

2 August:

Israeli troops move heavy artillery to front line through central Beirut.
Intermittent sniper fire between Palestinians and Israelis threatens to break
ninth ceasefire.
— Reagan sends birthday greetings to Begin.

3 August:

The last western ambassador left in West Beirut, the Canadian Theodore
Arcand, is ordered to leave by his government for his own safety.
— Senior UN official complains that UN observers, UNIFIL troops and relief
workers are being turned back from border of occupied Lebanon by Israelis.
Accusation denied by Israeli military spokesman.
— Israeli foreign minister Yitzhak Shamir publicly snubbed by Reagan in
Washington as sign of displeasure at heavy bombardments which it is
claimed disrupt Habib's negotiations.

4–5 August:

Heaviest bombardment to date over Palestinian areas and Hamra. Police
department reports 250 civilian dead on 4 August alone. In East Beirut, 50
reported dead as Israeli guns, placed near civilian installations (as the
Palestinian guns are in West Beirut), attract return fire.
— Heaviest Israeli losses to date: 19 soldiers die on 4 August. *The Times*
estimates that in 4 days, 30,000 have left West Beirut, while 400,000 remain.

5 August:

Israel estimates cost of war to date at £1000m.
— Mild appeal from US for Israel to pull back troops from central Beirut and
warning that military supplies could be affected.

6 August:

150 die in an 8-floor building struck by bomb.

8 August:

Regional Red Cross director John Desalis warns that West Beirut is 'on verge
of epidemic'.
— Drinking water restored after two weeks. Electricity still cut off so the
water cannot be pumped out of reservoir except by using 10 generators
supplied by UNICEF.
— PLO expresses willingness for evacuation, 'given that the Arab regimes
have not lifted a finger to help them' (David Hirst in *The Guardian*), but only
on condition that the evacuation starts as the first contingent of the multinational force arrives. Begin insists that 6–8,000 guerrillas must leave before
the multinational force arrives.

9 August:

Seven-hour air and artillery bombardment of West Beirut refugee camps
after Israelis claim Palestinians have been firing from the mountains on
Israeli armoury in East Beirut.
108 — Paris: 6 die in attack on Jewish restaurant.

Monday, 9 August 1982:
IN THE DESERTED CHATILA CAMP

The Palestinian camp of Chatila is deserted. The shack is stacked with weapons: Kalashnikovs, RPG rocket launchers, grenades, and also damaged machine guns and sub-machine guns taken from the enemy.

The fighter who greets us is not the kind of Palestinian that you meet in the company of someone from the PLO press office. He makes no passionate declarations about the resistance by Chatila camp, or the inevitability of final victory. He has an air of reserve, a tough nut to crack. The go-between who introduces me is one of his friends, a militant in one of the parties making up the National Movement.

We begin our tour of the camp. Under the midday sun, the crickets hidden among the pine trees are making a devilish racket. Little alleyways snake betwen the one-storey houses. The sand gets into your shoes. The houses are made of breezeblocks or corrugated iron, topped off by makeshift roofs that are held in place by the weight of old tyres or stones to prevent them blowing away. The refugees have left the camp in order to find new refuge in the centre of Beirut. Before leaving they have locked their doors with small padlocks whose security value is more symbolic than real. The whole camp suggests absence. On the ground lie empty food tins, empty Pepsi cans, a book in Arabic, squashed by a piece of shrapnel. A little further on, pages from an abandoned duplicated copy of the Lebanese constitution are blowing down the road.

A thousand little tell-tale signs reveal that the camp's inhabitants did what they could to turn this jumble of rambling shacks into a semblance of home. Some of the walls have been painted with slightly childish wall-paintings, in which the colour blue stands out. In more than one doorway there are empty powdered milk tins filled with earth. The heat of the August sun has dried out the plants that were growing in them. The bougainvilleas that climb up the fronts of some houses, and the rubber trees peeping over the tops of walls seem to have survived better; the overhanging grapevines too.

There are graffiti everywhere. 'Fatah' is painted on walls, but the names and symbols of other Palestinian organisations also appear. Here and there yellowing photographs of Palestinian martyrs look down on you. The slogans and writings are not only political: 'House for sale. Apply here after four o'clock' says one; and another, in English, 'I Love You', next to a heart with an arrow through it.

'This was my house,' explains the fighter to whom we have been introduced. He points to a small pile of debris. The shacks are so fragile that a single mortar shell landing nearby is sufficient to demolish two or three at one go.

As we reach the main street of the camp, four or five metres wide, our guide stops us from going any further.

'Don't move,' he says. 'You're in their line of fire. Come behind this wall and look. You see that building at the end, about a kilometre down the road. That's where "they" are. Those are their positions.'

'What are they doing?'

'They've just finished building their defences. They have settled themselves in and moved up their artillery.'

'Were you here during the bombardments last Wednesday?'

'Yes. When they start shelling the camp, there's only one thing to do: head in the direction of the Israeli lines. You have to get as close to them as possible. Then they can't shoot at you, for fear of hitting their own soldiers.'

On the other side of the street a man appears, dressed in civilian clothes. The fighter explains that for the last two days the refugees have been sending one of their number to keep an eye on the camp to see if their houses are still standing. The man shouts out: 'Is it OK to cross the street?'

'Watch out,' replies our guide. ' "They" have got snipers on the job all the time. If you want to get across, you'd better run.'

The man does not wait around. He sprints across the few metres of road separating us. No sound of bullets. Only the never-ending noise of crickets.

We continue with our visit. The alleyway broadens out. Two wrecked cars have been abandoned at the corner of the street. One has been hit by a shell; the other has run over a mine. Both their petrol tanks have their tops off, and a piece of tubing hangs from one of them. The fighters have siphoned off the petrol. There is a fuel shortage.

At the camp exit we come across a gathering of people. A bomb dropped by a plane three days previously has fractured a water pipe. The bomb crater has turned into a little pond, and the whole neighbourhood comes here to get water. Women squat and wash clothes, and then move off with their big tubs balanced on their heads. Others hold cans under the bits of water-piping sticking out to collect drinking water. Fighters strip down to their underwear and immerse themselves in the water. We sit down a little way off, smoking cigarettes and watching people come and go. After all, since the dawn of time, watering spots have been the place where people have met and made contact. Even our reserved fighter has become a little more talkative.

'I was born in a village not far from Nablus, on the West Bank. I arrived in Lebanon in 1975.'

'Will you be involved in the evacuation of the 10,000 fighters from Beirut?'

'In principle, only those who arrived in 1948 and 1967 have the right to remain.'

'So are you willing to leave?'

'I haven't yet packed my bags, but I shall follow the orders given by the leaders of my organisation, Fatah. If they tell me to go, then, yes, I shall go . . .'

(Beirut, 9 August 1982)

Guarding the Galerie Semaan cross-over point from West to East Beirut

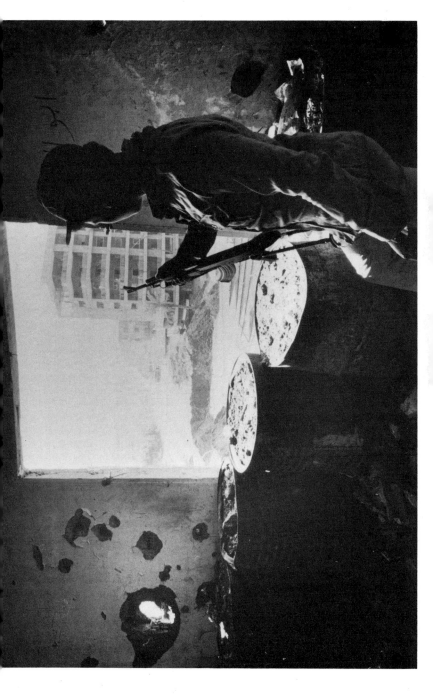

10 August:
Israeli bombardment badly damages the synagogue in West Beirut and houses in Wadi Abu Jamil where a community of about 50 elderly Jews live. — PLO fighters force Israeli troops into retreat near Museum crossing.

Tuesday, 10 August 1982: IN BOURJ AL-BRAJNEH

In the high-ceilinged basement of a building on the outskirts of the camp, Palestinian women sit in a circle on mats on the ground. Old women, mothers, hardly visible in the darkness, recognisable only by their long white scarves.

One of them smokes a *nargileh*; another blows on charcoal. A camping-gas lamp in the middle of the circle lights up the scene and casts long shadows against the wall. The surrounding concrete pillars create areas of intimacy.

When I ask how things have been going, and whether they suffered badly in the bombings of Wednesday night, a white-haired woman takes me on an underground tour, leading me by the hand. She realises that my eyes have not yet adjusted from the daylight outside. We stop in front of a little pile of cinders. She tells me to look up. Through a hole in the roof you can see a small area of light. 'The shell came in through there. A phosphorous shell. But we were able to put it out.'

She leads me on. We pass the exist from the basement area, a gentle slope going up to the outside world. A slightly orange light filters through suspended dust. At the bottom of the ramp a girl sits with a baby in her arms.

We continue on our way, her in front and me behind. The basements of the buildings are intercommunicating. Suddenly we enter another cellar. Once again, pillars, and yet another world peopled by white-scarved ghosts sitting in a circle.

When we get back to our own circle a few minutes later, a lively discussion is under way. The women are wondering whether the fighters – that is, their children – will be able to leave Beirut safe and sound, or whether the Israeli army will try to attack the city and slaughter them.

'Does the evacuation involve you?'

'In principle, no,' replies one of the women. 'The *fedayeen* who have to leave are those who came to Lebanon after 1967. We are refugees from 1948, we are Lebanese Palestinians. But some fighters, the children of the 1948 refugees, will also have to leave. And they won't be able to take their families with them . . .'

Another woman chimes in: 'Bourj al-Brajneh itself dates from 1948. When we arrived there was nothing here but sand and jackals. The Palestinians built this camp with their own hands. They built house after house with money hard-earned by fathers, brothers and sons who had emigrated to 112 Kuwait, Saudi Arabia, Qatar and Dubai. I remember how it was in my house; we never opened the windows at the back, so as not to hear the jackals howling in the night. Let me tell you, money didn't grow on trees in this place.'

'Everything that you see here,' explains a third woman, 'the whole of Bourj al-Brajneh, has taken an entire lifetime to build, to raise it from the sand. We had to scrimp and save to get a few belongings, buy a few pieces of furniture.'

She waves her hand around her, as if to say that, for her, the Palestinian camp was heaven on earth.

'Everything that we have built,' says another, 'everything that we have done over the last 34 years, has been destroyed by the Israelis in this war. They want to scatter us yet again. We're used to it. But the children who have been born here, who have never known any other country but this, for whom Bourj al-Brajneh, despite everything, is home . . . how are they going to be able to leave?'

Coffee is served. Young lads bring it in and run out again. The tray is passed round; the *nargilehs* too. Silence reigns. The Lebanese friend who brought me here explains to the assembled company that, in his opinion, the Israelis will move onto the offensive, on the one hand in order to annihilate the PLO, but also in order to instal in Beirut a regime favourable to themselves. The Palestinians listen religiously.

'Israel,' he explains, 'wants to see a puppet president installed, who can then sign a peace treaty. Then a set of unequal economic relations will be set up. Already Israeli agricultural produce is invading our markets. I have seen seven- or eight-centimetre cucumbers, completely tasteless, in the markets. The sort of cucumbers that we would never grow. And I've seen apples . . .

'Yes,' one of the young women interrupts, dreamily, 'I've seen apples too.' She makes a gesture as if she is holding one in her hand. She lifts it up as if to smell it. 'They're Israeli apples. But they're also Palestinian apples. I have smelt them. I recognised those apples. They come from the village of Telchiha.'

(Bourj al-Brajneh, 10 August 1982)

12 August:

Ten-hour bombardment of Sabra-Chatila and Bourj al-Brajneh camps. Lebanese police figures of deaths in Beirut since invasion: 3,983 plus 'several hundred' from 12 August raids, and in all Lebanon: 11,492.

— Split Israeli cabinet calls halt to bombing as Sharon outvoted. Reagan warns Begin ceasefire must hold. Begin still objects to inclusion of French army in multinational force, because of 'rampant anti-Semitism' in France, and to inclusion of UN observers.

— Douglas Hurd, minister of state at the Foreign Office in London, expresses concern at level of civilian deaths 'in pursuit of objectives which are very far from clear and probably not going to be realised.' In a radio interview he says the PLO are not going to be destroyed. 'They are going to move to Damascus, to Syria and to other Arab countries, and I think the historian will find it very odd so many people should have been killed for that purpose. The Palestinian cause, the idea that the Palestinians deserve a homeland, is not going to be destroyed because a number of Palestinians are killed in Lebanon. The problem is going to persist until it is solved.'

Thursday, 12 August 1982: CEASEFIRES MEAN NOTHING TO THE ISRAELIS

Israel's murderous bombings continue. Their pilots take off from airports in northern Israel and, within minutes, they are over the besieged Lebanese capital. They carry out a dummy run over their designated targets. Behind them they drop regularly spaced decoy flares, designed to draw the anti-aircraft fire of the SAM missiles. Then they come over on a second run. The computer on board activates the plane's firing mechanism, and it drops its lethal load. Several tonnes of metal drop to earth, blasting buildings, killing and mutilating people, and tearing up the ground.

At ground level you can hear the explosions over the roar of the jet engines. The Palestinians' anti-aircraft batteries respond but to little effect. The pilots continue their dance of death until they have exhausted their ammunition. Then they head back southwards. On the way back they pass more laden bombers en route to take over from them. And so it goes on. From 6 a.m. to the end of the day the skies over Beirut are hardly empty for a moment.

The Israelis' naval guns and land artillery have also played their part. The four Palestinian camps in the southern part of the city have been hit again and again. Sabra, Chatila, Bourj al-Brajneh and Mar Elias. Leaving aside any political or military considerations, it seems that Israel is pursuing a policy of destruction for its own sake. The camps in southern Lebanon have been bulldozed. Now, the camps in Beirut are being systematically destroyed. Israel's intention is that, by the end of this war, the Palestinians should have no roof over their heads. The Israelis work methodically.

The inner circle areas of the city have not been spared either. Corniche al-Mazraa; the avenue leading to the TV station; UNESCO; Verdun; Ramleth; Baida; the Murr tower . . . It would be a lot quicker to list the areas which have *not* been hit – a small section of the city centre. Fighting has been going on at the Museum crossing, and there are contradictory reports coming in about the taking of the Beirut hippodrome. The artillery of the Palestinian and progressive forces has responded by shelling various parts of East Beirut and the Christian areas.

Forty-eight air raids over Beirut on Thursday
Many of the Palestinian refugees from the deserted camps have taken shelter in the two-storey basement of Beirut's shopping centre, the 'Concorde'. Two thousand people, mostly women and children, are crammed together in this small space. The heat and the smell are dreadful. As the aircraft continue their dance of death in the skies overhead, the refugees huddle together in a darkness that is broken only where a solitary candle provides the light for whole families.

The 'Concorde' has become the main gathering point for the city's refugees; it has taken in the people previously occupying schools and the public parks which were last week bombarded by the Israelis. In one corner of the basement, I am introduced to one of the young people in charge of civil defence. Today he is organising the shopping centre area, but yesterday he was a fighter with the PFLP (Popular Front for the Liberation of Palestine). He gives me the figures for the number of refugees, and describes the problems of keeping them supplied with food. Then he continues: 'Yes, it's true, we'll soon be leaving Beirut. These past few years we have dedicated ourselves mainly to the political struggle. In this war we have seen how the Arab countries have behaved towards us . . . Soon we are going to be scattered to the four corners of the world. And then we are going to put our political work to one side. They call us terrorists? Fine. Soon, our hour of revenge will come.'

(Beirut, 12 August 1982)

Friday, 13 August 1982: ROOTING OUT AN IDEA

Friday the 13th. Seventieth day of the war; sixty-ninth day of the siege. The city woke up this morning, to complete calm. A normal, peaceful summer's day. Those daily newspapers which are still appearing published several pages showing the destruction and the horrors of yesterday. Scenes of everyday life in the summer of 1982.

The people of Beirut are beyond anger and indignation. The city is in the 115 grip of a kind of gloomy fatalism, a feeling that everything is useless. The Palestinians had just agreed to a whole set of concessions; only a few points of detail remained to be tidied up. But still the planes of death came back, dropping their bombs on a virtually unarmed population. They come with impunity, in order to kill and maim.

A shrug of the shoulders greets the moral outrage of the outside world. Reactions are half-hearted as people hear of the disagreements within the Israeli cabinet, the belated anger of President Reagan, and the Security Council resolution calling for the lifting of the blockade of Beirut.

For the people of Beirut, it's all just wind and piss. They have come to understand their deadly enemy. They have seen an unaccountable complacency on the part of the Americans and a semi-passivity of the European countries which has permitted the Israelis to do what they like. Was the Argentinians' action in attacking the Malvinas islands any more serious a crime than Israel invading Lebanon? The people of West Beirut would be happy if only half the sanctions applied against the Argentinians were also applied against Israel. Fat chance!

People don't dwell on this too much. They're too preoccupied with trying to organise their survival. Yesterday, deliveries of tomatoes, aubergines and grapes managed to get through the blockade. The prices vary between 15 and 25 Lebanese pounds per kilo (9 Lebanese pounds = £1 sterling). There's not enough power to raise water above the ground floor of houses even in the low-lying areas of the city. Electricity is a thing of the past. Food is beginning to be in short supply. As for health, the doctors are describing the situation as alarming. With so many refugees packed into the city centre, if an epidemic breaks out, it will very soon prove catastrophic . . .

It may well be that, as politically aware people are saying, the policy of the Begin government is leading Israel into disaster. Perhaps Begin will pay for all this one day. However, this is only true in the long term. For the moment, families are shattered beyond repair, a city is half destroyed, and as before, a people is condemned once again to diaspora.

People are confused by Israel's apparent determination. In a way this has been a strange war. Israel invaded Lebanon and is destroying its capital in order to kill an *idea* – the idea of the existence of a Palestinian people. This show of strength has been fundamental for Israel. It is by this means that Israel hopes to become one of the world's important countries. Leaving aside all political and military calculations, this war has an almost metaphysical aspect. In order to exist, one has to make the other disappear. The problem is that this disappearance can only be symbolic. Whatever may be said by those who have lost their sense of proportion, the Israelis as a nation are not unanimous about this war. They are not capable of the physical liquidation of an entire people. Therefore, the annihilation will be essentially in moral terms.

What more can one say? The Palestinians have no land, nothing that belongs to them in their own right. They have nothing that can be held to ransom, to force them into an agreement. All they have is an idea in their

Israeli bombardment of West Beirut

heads, the idea that they are a nation. How can this idea be rooted out? All that you can force them to do is to disperse. The law of the jungle rules. But military force and metaphysics have always made bad bedfellows. Metaphysics plays tricks, and it can sometimes end by turning things into their opposite. Remember the parable of the 'last who shall be first . . .'

By refusing to evacuate Beirut until now, the Palestinians have shown that they are not about to disappear. On the contrary. Beirut may be worn out, bled dry, and subjected to a daily pounding, but its Lebanese and Palestinian population is still holding out. Faced with an Arab world that is powerless and defeated, this resistance of the weak has become a challenge for the future. From tomorrow, who will dare say that the Palestinian people is not a reality?

(Beirut, 13 August 1982)

14 August:
Mother Teresa of Calcutta evacuates 37 handicapped children from a bombed mental home in Sabra to the school in East Beirut which she opened in 1980.

15 August:
Arafat thanks King Fahd of Saudi Arabia for persuading Reagan to call for a halt to the bombardments. The Saudis had claimed the credit for Reagan's angry phone call to Begin on 12 August.

17 August:
Israeli troops hand over the parliament building to Lebanese army.
— Begin expresses shock at Mitterrand's statement 'The PLO has earned a right to fight [for a homeland].'

17–20 August
Relative peace for the first time in 2½ months, as arrangements for arrival of multinational force and evacuation of PLO continue.

Arrangements of multinational force subject to continuous change but announced as:
800 US marines with an additional 1000 in reserve on offshore ships
800 French troops
400 Italian troops

Friday, 20 August 1982: PRIDE, MODESTY AND MOCK LEATHER SUITCASES

There are three of them. They are recognisable by their accents, not very different from the Lebanese accent, but with inflections and turns of phrase that are typically Palestinian.

'How much is this big suitcase?'

The street-seller answers mechanically. His wares are spread out across a five-metre stretch of pavement: suitcases of all sizes, all colours, made of mock-leather or stout cardboard. Cheap suitcases.

'And the middle one, how much is that?'

This transaction does not take long. For several days now business has been brisk, and competition severe. All over town, street vendors have been popping up. The three men hand over their money, and go off down the street. Suitcase on one shoulder, and Kalashnikov on the other.

Things go on pretty much as normal. The women stand in an orderly queue at the entrance of the refugee aid office. An everyday routine for the volunteers in charge. While one of them writes down names and checks their papers, another hands over food (sugar, lentils, powdered milk, etc.), and a third fills cooking pots with margarine. A very everyday scene – but, as she goes out, one of the women turns round. She too is recognisable by her accent.

'I would just like to say,' she says in a low voice, 'that this is the last time I shall be coming for supplies. Next week we will have gone.'

The aid committee has never differentiated between Palestinian and Lebanese refugees. Food distribution has never been segregated. But the woman's words suddenly draw a dividing line between those who are leaving and those who will stay. Just before disappearing, she adds; 'I wanted to thank you for everything you've done.'

Outside the PLO's press office, a number of men are taking the air. Their chairs form a circle in the road. On the ground, yet another suitcase – filled to bursting, and tied together with string. Its owner explains that he had tiny fragments of shrapnel in his eye; he's had one operation, and is hoping that a second operation will restore his sight to normal. But first he must leave for Greece.

On the balcony of a first-floor flat where they have been living since the start of the war, a dozen young Palestinians have gathered. For two and a half months they have lived the same lives, shared the same risks together.

'Myself,' says one of them, 'I was born in Bourj al-Brajneh. My parents came there in 1948. I'm staying in Lebanon. What the future holds, I have no idea. Whether Gemayel wins the presidency of the republic, or someone else, it's not going to be easy for us. There's certain to be repression. I shall try to return to my studies, and to start a new life. But I shall still remain a member of Fatah. I think that our conditions of struggle are going to be very 119 different. We are going to have to organise clandestinely . . . But the truth is that none of us knows what's going to happen. What guarantees do we have?'

Another joins in: 'I was born in Jordan. I arrived in Lebanon in 1970, after Hussein declared war on us. I have not set foot in Jordan since. How is the Jordanian government going to treat us when we arrive? I have no idea. But we have no choice. We have to leave. At least I'll be seeing my relations again, and the places where I grew up . . .'

'It's still sad, though,' says another of those present. 'I'm in the Palestine Liberation Army [PLA], in a unit of the Syrian contingent of the Arab Deterrent Force. But don't think that I support the Assad government. It's just that I grew up in Syria, and I have to go back there. I was very young when I joined Fatah. Then, when I had to do my military service, I joined the PLA. Now I'm going to be evacuated to Damascus. They've told us that we'll get a rest period for three months or so, and then we'll come back to Lebanon, in the Bekaa valley . . .'

'If the Syrian forces are still there,' someone butts in.

Someone else takes up the theme: 'Militarily, we succeeded in holding off the Israelis. They were not able to take a single one of our positions. Look at all our positions around Beirut: the airport, the Chehab barracks in the southern suburbs, the military courts at the Museum crossing. Where positions were over-run, it was thanks to the complicity of the Lebanese army. But the Israelis have shown that they would have no hesitations about destroying Beirut. And we have shown that we would not let it be demolished. There lies the whole difference . . .'

One of them is leaving for Cairo; another for Tunis; a third is going to Amman, and another to Sanaa. Already they are beginning to live for tomorrow. They're still together, but they're already, in a sense, apart. The Israelis' war has not only created a division between Lebanese and Palestinians: it has also divided the Palestinians, by countries of destination.

Everything is ready for D-day – this August 21st which will go down in history as the end of the Israeli–Palestinian part of the war. The final obstacle – the handing over of two Israeli prisoners and the bodies of nine dead Israeli soldiers – was sorted out on Friday. The evacuees have been preparing discreetly for their departure. There is unhappiness at leaving. But pride, and the ever-present threat of an enemy ready to pounce at the slightest sign of weakness, prevents them from showing it. They know that they have lost a battle. They recognise that they have been hit. Even if hundreds of thousands of Palestinians will be remaining in Lebanon (and probably thousands of fighters among them), the PLO's time in Lebanon is drawing to an end. The Palestinians are losing a sanctuary, though their honour is preserved and their leadership remains intact.

The problem with historic events is that when they happen, they seem already to belong to the past. At 5 a.m., in the port of Beirut, now emptied of Israeli troops, 350 French paratroopers arrive. They are the vanguard of the multinational intervention force. Six hours later, the first 50 PLO fighters to be evacuated embark on a Greek ship bound for Cyprus. All of a sudden it seems like a play, which has to reach a conclusion and must 120 provide a symbol for what has happened, for an action that is past and gone.

In private, the Palestinians are sad and worried. One more time they must pack their bags. Yet again, they pick up their bundles. They are the region's new Wandering Jews. As for the Beirutis, they are becoming increasingly worried about what is going to happen once the PLO leaves. At the Semaan and Museum crossing points, the Lebanese army has moved in to replace the Israelis. Anyone who has returned to West Beirut in the past few days has found, to their surprise, that Lebanon's army, where it has control of the barricades, has been continuing and maintaining the blockade of the city even more effectively, in some instances, than the occupying forces themselves. A few lorryloads of fruit and vegetables have been allowed to pass – as can be seen from greengrocers' shops in the besieged city. But there are reports of bags of bread, ready-cooked meals and food carried by pedestrians being thrown to the ground by over-zealous guards at the crossing points. This scene has been repeated so many times that it simply cannot be a matter of 'individual excesses'. The news spread through the city like wildfire. The message was clear. In the words of a hall porter from a block of flats: 'If the soldiers are behaving like this even before they've reached Beirut, then what are they going to be like when they arrive? By their behaviour, they are making it obvious that they are not coming in a spirit of national reconciliation; they are coming to smash us. They don't seem to appreciate the fact that we have put up resistance while they themselves have not fired a single shot at the invaders.'

On Wednesday, Thursday and today, booby-trapped cars were left in the streets of Beirut. The first one exploded and injured four people. The other two were defused in time. The second contained 200 kilos of Israeli-made explosives. It had come from East Beirut that same morning.

So, it is not only for sentimental reasons that the people of the besieged capital view the departure of the Palestinians on their ships with apprehension. Seen from Beirut, Lebanon is a wholly occupied country: 65 per cent occupied by the Israeli army, and the rest by the Syrians. The 2,130 men of the multinational force, whose mandate is limited to 30 days, will be able to provide only limited protection. As the Palestinians start to take their leave, Beirut fears that it will be punished for having welcomed them in the first place, and for having stood up when everyone expected it to lie down.

(Beirut, 20 August 1982)

20 August:
Announcement of Palestinian and allied units to be evacuated under the plan agreed by the PLO and the Israelis through Philip Habib.

21 August:
After the handing over of two Israeli prisoners, demanded as an extra condition by Begin, PLO evacuation begins and continues for the next 15 days.

Sunday, 22 August 1982: FAREWELL TO BEIRUT

Evacuation schedule
3,500 members of Fatah
800 members of Saiqa
650 members of PDFLP
600 members of PFLP
550 members of PFLP-GC
550 members of ALF
900 members of PLF and PSF

Members of the Palestine Liberation Army (PLA) to return to their respective countries:
2,000 to Syria
1,000 to Egypt
800 to Iraq
600 to various other Arab countries

1,000 PLO foreign volunteers, mainly from Bangladesh, India and Pakistan to leave by sea
1,000 Syrian troops will evacuate by land to the Bekaa valley

It all began when the gates of the municipal stadium opened and the first lorries of the military convoy emerged. At once a barrage of gunfire resounded, accompanied by the sound of cheering and weeping – the expressions of anger and solidarity. Thousands of hands reached skywards in a defiant V-for-victory salute: a sign of victory, but also a promise that the struggle will continue. Until this point, people had managed to contain their emotions – passionate anger, sadness, and love towards those who were leaving them. Up until that point, the scenario planned by the PLO – for a dignified evacuation, a disciplined retreat, in new uniforms – had been more or less respected. But in the event, emotions proved too strong.

On the first lorry to appear, the fighters stood, displaying Palestinian and Lebanese flags, a portrait of Yasser Arafat and their Kalashnikovs. The dam of pent-up feeling broke. The crowd moved and surged as one, reaching out to the men on the lorry. Waves of movement ran through them. They leaned and swayed as if drunk, shouting at the tops of their voices over and over again words which you could only understand by lip-reading, so deafening was the din. The noise of gunfire was painful to the ears, almost unbearable; the smell of gunpowder was overpowering; cart-

Traumatised children after Israeli bombardment had destroyed their
dormitory in Lebanese mental hospital, West Beirut

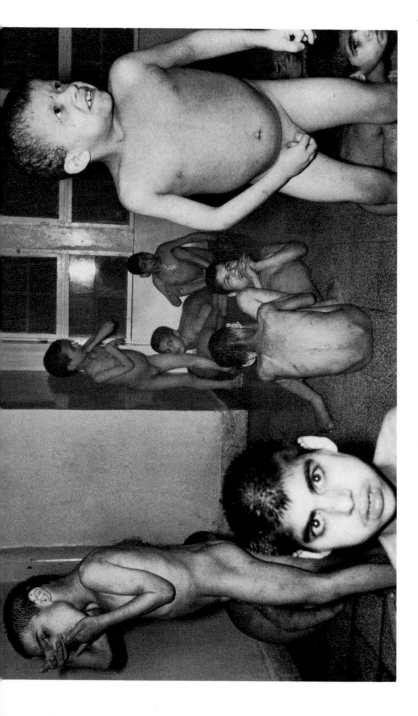

ridge cases ejected from firing Kalashnikovs fell on an unheeding crowd. *Allah maakone! Allah Yihfazone!, Ma al salameh!* ['God be with you!', 'God protect you!' and 'Go in peace!'], the women shouted, their voices cracked and broken, their eyes red with crying and their faces twisted with sorrow. The men, too, were crying. A lad of 15 years struggled up the side of the lorry. He kissed his friends on both cheeks, four times, as per tradition. He hugged them as he passed up bottles of water.

Another deafening salvo greets the appearance of the second and third lorries. The *fedayeen* are garlanded with frangipani flowers intertwined with their black and white *kouffiyehs*. One of them wears the Palestinian flag draped round his shoulders. Another has a determined and slightly abstract look as he waves goodbye. Yet another fires his gun, emptying an entire magazine, as if the sky itself, the whole world were to blame.

A few metres down the road, a man slips and bangs his head on a car bonnet. He utters an uncontrolled torrent of curses and abuse, not knowing whom to blame. Around him, Palestinian women make no attempt to conceal the tears rolling down their cheeks. They are all dressed in black. The emotion is so intense that even some of the journalists present look visibly upset and tearful. I saw some cameramen who could not bring themselves to film the scene – at such moments the intrusion of the voyeur would have seemed indecent . . .

It's only now that I realise that I have never seen the Palestinians gathered together in such great numbers. Usually they only show themselves in small groups of four or five, ten at the most. They don't even gather in large numbers on the war front, having always operated as guerrilla forces. Nor did I ever see them surrounded by their families. Now, as they make their final preparations for departure, I discover that they have mothers, sisters, wives and children . . .

'When you get to Amman, tell Aunt So-and-so that Walid and Mahmoud have been imprisoned by the Israelis. Tell her to do what she can from her end . . . Tell her that we're in very good health here . . . Look after yourself . . . God protect you.'

Anger and mourning

A woman, aged around 50. Holding back her emotions, she manages to keep her composure as she hugs her son to her breast. But when he begins to strap on his backpack, her feelings overwhelm her. She cries on his shoulder. Then she tries to pull herself together. She blows her nose noisily. Another mother has found cans of Pepsi on sale at the stadium entrance. She buys two and empties them into the water bottle hanging from her son's belt. This scene is being repeated all over the stadium. Small though they are, these last minute attentions – a packet of biscuits or a carton of cigarettes slipped into a fighter's backpack, some fruit, or a word of advice – convey a love and depth of feeling that finds no other way to express itself.

The scene has the appearance of troops leaving for the front. Men in full combat gear, armed to the teeth, with their packs slung over one shoulder. Families bustling around in all directions, their minds taken up with their loved ones, their sons and brothers who are leaving. Soon, when they are perched on top of their lorries, these sons and brothers will merge in a sea of indistinct faces, cheered as they go and showered with rice and the blessings of loving mothers.

A group of young fighters, whose large light blue suitcases look odd among the military packs surrounding them, tell me: 'We held out for 79 days. A lot longer than any Arab country. We held out for 79 days in the hope that something would happen, that the paralysed Arab world would finally come out of its lethargy, would gather its forces, and would react. A waste of time. The Arab world is fucked. So, since we can expect nothing from them, since this is the way it is, we have no choice but to leave . . . But this is only a postponement.'

Two departing fighters pose for the camera of a cousin who is staying behind. They stand still, looking straight into the camera, one of them with his arm round the other. They are representative of their people: Palestinians about to depart, forced into new wanderings; Palestinians dispersed, chased from Beirut, but by no means broken; Palestinians in arms . . .

The convoy begins to move off. The city opens up before it, for a last farewell. Men, women and children are gathered all along the roadside. They raise the V-for-victory sign, and shout aloud: *Saura, Saura, hatta al Nasr!* ('Revolution! Revolution, until victory!'). This Fatah slogan is virtually synonymous with the Palestinian revolution. It is found at the bottom of all PLO correspondence, even on credentials issued to journalists. But this time the familiar, almost routine slogan takes on the quality of a quietly voiced declaration of war. Once again, people's voices can hardly be heard above the rattle of gunfire that accompanies the convoy on its way. Gradually the firing spreads through the whole city. Now it's not just Kalashnikovs. Other guns join in: heavy machine guns, anti-aircraft guns, and artillery. This deafening din is the city's salute to the departing PLO fighters. So much for the advice given earlier, that people should not fire off their guns because it's dangerous and because it wastes ammunition. Once again, the dam of pent-up emotion has broken. Hundreds of thousands of bullets are fired in honour of the evacuees. And the children run to pick up the cartridge cases from the ground where they have fallen.

A last farewell

By now the convoy has reached the Fakhani district: half destroyed and three quarters deserted. There are still women on the balconies, showering the passing convoy with handfuls of rice. On the pavements, the men gather in a guard of honour for the fighters, to give them heart and tell them that they will not be forgotten. Mazraa too, the Sunni quarter of Beirut, salutes the travellers. The Nasserites of the Morabitoun are in full battle dress. They too pay their respects, firing off volley after volley.

The convoy passes through the various quarters of Beirut. Mar Elias, with its Catholics, is no less warm and welcoming than the others. The militia of the Progressive Socialist Party (Jumblatt's party) welcome the convoy in Caracol al-Druze. Then the Kurds in Wadi Abu Jamil, Beirut's ancient Jewish quarter. A little further on, it is the turn of the soldiers of the Syrian 85 Brigade, under their commander Mohamed Halal, seen as hero 125 because of his conduct in the fighting around the airport. The crowds are sometimes so dense that the convoy is forced to stop. Here and there banners and posters are waved. Some are written in English or French: 'Sharon = Nero', 'All Roads Lead to Jerusalem', 'Beirut is Proud of You'. Most, though, are in Arabic: 'Beirut Salutes the Palestinian Heroes', 'Beirut, the Resistance, Salutes You', 'From Today, No More Talk of Arabism'. This last banner also has insults questioning the virtue of the wives and sisters of the Arab nations . . .

I am no longer an Arab

The Arabs. They are the main target for the anger of those who are leaving and those who stay behind. The anger is not directed against Israel. Israel is the enemy, and has behaved as such. It is on their self-styled 'brothers' that the anger of Beirutis is focused.

Standing on the back of one of the lorries, a fighter curses the Arab nations at the top of his voice, with all the force he can muster, with all the hatred in his heart. 'I am not an Arab!' he shouts. 'I am not an Arab! I am only a Palestinian!'

He bawls himself utterly hoarse, and yet manages to make himself heard over the gunfire. His words are taken up by the swaying crowd, and feed their anger, and their fury.

A photographer steps forward. As he gets the man in his viewfinder, brandishing his portrait of Arafat in one hand, the man suddenly turns round and bends over: 'You want to photograph me? Go on then . . . photograph my arse!'

The convoy heads for the seashore at Zeitoune, the old quarter once famed for its night-life, but now lying demolished and deserted. We are approaching the ruined shells of the big hotels. A few hundred metres further on is the entry to the harbour, solidly guarded by a phalanx of French legionnaires and Lebanese soldiers. This is the moment of separation. The crowd is not allowed to accompany the fighters any further. Any remaining ammunition is fired in thundering volleys. Hand grenades are hurled, to explode on a nearby mound of rubble. This frenzy reaches its climax as the lorries pass through the lines of soldiers and disappear into the port enclosure. The men wave their arms in a final farewell.

Sunday is the second day of the evacuation. The crowd is even bigger than the day before. Unless the Israelis have a change of heart, the evacuation will continue like this, every day, for the coming two weeks. Not content with having chased them out of their homes and expropriating their lands, the Israelis have even pursued the Palestinians into the countries where they have sought refuge, in order to drive them still further off. However, though the expulsions are powerful symbols, particularly the expulsion of the PLO leadership, they are by no means massive. Hundreds of thousands of Palestinians will remain in Lebanon, just as they remain in Syria, in Jordan, in Egypt, in the Gulf, and in the entire world . . .

After the battle of Beirut, these Palestinians feel themselves more Palestinian than ever. The Israeli government is under a delusion if it believes that they will resign themselves either to accepting integration into the Arab nations who have let them down so badly, or to participating in any Camp David agreement which gives them merely administrative autonomy on the West Bank.

It was in the aftermath of the 1948 defeat that a revival of nationalism brought down one Arab government after another. The long battle of Beirut, and the way it has resolved itself in the absence of any Arab state presence, may prove more explosive still. If such a nationalist movement emerges anew, it will take the example of the besieged Lebanese capital as its starting point. The image of the armed Palestinians, crowded into lorries and driving through the ruins of a half-destroyed city, to the thunderous applause of the city's people, will not be forgotten. Israel has sown the wind . . .

(Beirut, 22 August 1982)

23 August:
Bashir Gemayel, Phalangist leader, elected president of Lebanon.

Friday, 27 August 1982:
PARTY FOR A PALESTINIAN WHO IS LEAVING FOR NOWHERE

By the sixth day, the Palestinians' farewell drive through the city and the last honours that accompany them, has become routine. A kilo of cartridge cases fetches 1 Lebanese pound (11 pence) at the local bullet factory. The accompanying gunfire guarantees that the daily departure of the Palestinians leaves its mark on the city.

There are other, less obvious, rituals of the evacuation of the city. Every evening, throughout West Beirut, the Palestinians who are due to leave the following day gather with their friends, neighbours and brothers-in-arms for a *haslet wiya*, a farewell party.

Some of these are boisterous, semi-public events. They generally take place in one of the little streets of the neighbourhood where the Palestinians have lived for the past 12 years – their 'Lebanese period'. We won't be seeing Abu Walid, Abu Mahmoud, or Abu Hicham again (unless we meet again some day in a free Palestine), so let's drink a toast to them. The Palestinians who arrived in 1948, by now half-Lebanese, will be staying on. The Orient has always saluted parting friends and relations with tears and emotional outbursts. For such a massive departure as this, the city is filled with spontaneously organised farewells, full of regrets and eternal hope.

Abu Hani's last night in Beirut
Some farewells are more intimate, more subdued. Abu Hani sits at a neatly laid table on the balcony of a Christian family in West Beirut. He is a 127

mid-ranking officer in the Palestine Liberation Army (PLA). He's in his forties, wears a traditional *kouffiyeh* on his head, and sports a neat, freshly trimmed moustache. He's dressed in a not very military beige uniform, and carries no gun. He resembles anything but an officer of the PLA. And yet for the past few months he has been the military officer in charge of this neighbourhood. Slowly he has built up a friendship with the younger members of this particular family, who acted as volunteers in the neighbourhood's civil defence team. That explains why he has come to spend his last night in Beirut with them.

'I feel like a man saying goodbye to his nearest and dearest relations . . .'

'But where is your real family?'

He gives a deprecatory smile and shrugs his shoulders, to indicate that he doesn't know.

'Some of them are in Jordan; some in Syria, some in Saudi Arabia . . . I learnt that my mother died in 1972. But I don't know when, or where she's buried. As for my wife and children, I haven't had news from them for months. The last time a letter reached me, it was to tell me that my eldest daughter – she's 18 – was engaged, but that she couldn't marry because she had no identity papers.'

'How's that?'

'It's because we've always had to move on a bit quickly from the places that we were staying.

'I'm from the village of S. on the West Bank. Before 1967 we were under the sovereignty of Jordan. The king was saying that we had to build a powerful army in order to liberate Palestine. I believed him. I was ashamed of the way the whole world referred to the Palestinians as "refugees". Why refugees? And why weren't we doing anything to change our situation and return to our country? I told myself that the Palestinians had to prepare themselves to live in dignity. That was how I came to join the Jordanian army. That was in 1956 . . .'

'My first period of exile'

He breaks off, because the lady of the house tells him to eat his food before it gets cold. He obeys willingly. A moment later, he asks, 'Why do they always talk about the "Six Day War"? From what I saw, the June 1967 war didn't last six hours! A large part of the Jordanian army was made up of Palestinians, and many like myself had joined up in order to liberate our country. And instead of that . . . I remember some Palestinian junior officers cutting off all communication with their superior command in order not to have to obey orders to stop fighting. Obviously, it was a waste of time in the end. We lost that war, with a vengeance . . .

'Less than a year later, one of the Fatah groups engaged the Israeli army in armed confrontation in the battle of Karameh. For me, that battle was the real start of the Palestinian resistance. In a defeated Arab world a small group of men decided to show that it was possible to make a stand, that it

Israeli soldier jogging in occupied West Beirut

was not a matter of equipment, but of determination. This was when I experienced my first period of exile. I went to Jordan from the West Bank. I was still a member of the Jordanian army. And when some Palestinian friends came and asked me to help the revolution financially, I decided to donate one dinar per month. That was about a quarter of my income which, as I recall, was 4 dinars and 42 piastres.'

'But why you? Shouldn't all Palestinians have done the same?'

'I don't know. I think that I must be different to the rest. I'm not typical. For example, I don't go to the right or to the left; I say what I think. I'm outspoken, and that sometimes gets me into trouble. For example, there are two things that I feel ashamed of – even though many other people are proud of them. Namely, my gun and my rank. You will never see me in the street with a pistol showing at my belt. If I'm wearing a baggy shirt, the gun will be tucked inside. But even so, I still feel ashamed of it. The same goes for my rank. I really don't like people to know that I'm an army officer. Other people, I know, go around with five bodyguards in front, five behind and five on either side. But myself, I believe that an officer should be the humble servant of those in his charge.'

The lady of the house interrupts again and suggests that he finishes his meal. In the darkness enveloping the city you hear repeated volleys of single-shot sub machine gun fire. Above our heads, tracer bullets soar like shooting stars. One of the Palestinians' parties is obviously firing a farewell salute.

Abu Hani continues his story. He describes the repression that King Hussein launched against the Palestinians in September 1970: 'Some Palestinian soldiers were forced to desert, so as not to have to fire on their brothers. Others, who felt the guns of their Jordanian officers at their backs, fired into the air, and threw their hand grenades without pulling the pins out.' He himself came into the first category. At the end of the fighting, he fled to Syria, taking part of his family with him. What else could he do? He was a professional soldier. So he joined the PLA.

No identity, no country

'With each new period of exile,' he continues, 'the problems were the same. For example, how can I prove that my children really are my children? I don't have any documents. In the end I told the Syrian clerk: "You'll have to be satisfied with the fact that these children call me daddy." It might seem stupid, perhaps, but that's our problem. We don't have an identity. We have to keep moving on. And it's the same today – no papers, no identity, no country. Always refugees. Never belonging to anywhere. If this kind of life was liveable, then we would have fitted in with it . . .' Every now and then he stops me writing something in my note-pad. 'No, don't write that. They'll recognise me. That bit's not worth writing . . . I'm going to have to make sure that I fit in, in the country where I eventually end up. If I lay into them and then they catch up with me, where am I going to end up? I don't want to end up in the sea . . !'

At the same time, he insists that I write down what he has to say about a number of Arab leaders:

'I would like to say a word to Gaddafy, who advised us to commit suicide rather than leave Beirut. I would like to say that we didn't see hide nor hair of Libya's tanks and planes. And the SAM 9 missiles that he supplied us were worthless. And as for dear Mr Assad, president of Syria, may God help him, he withdrew his forces one after another. He didn't seem to want those he left behind in Lebanon. He didn't seem to mean business with his pilots either. The planes he sent were made of cardboard. I would like to ask him where his super new modern aircraft were when Beirut was burning . . .'

As for Beirut, Abu Hani does not say much about the period of his life spent in Lebanon. He says simply that the people of Lebanon, and the people of Beirut in particular, have given the Palestinian people more than all the Arab countries put together. He says that he doesn't know how to thank them. He doesn't even feel bad towards those Lebanese who are anti-Palestinian. He says that it breaks his heart to leave, that it's like separating body from soul.

(Beirut, 27 August 1982)

Monday, 30 August 1982: JOURNALISTS IN THEIR KOUFFIYEHS

Everything happened very fast. At 7.30 p.m. on Sunday, 16 hours before the *Atlantis* is due to leave Beirut, Mahmud Labadi, the PLO's press officer, informs four members of the international press (a three-person television team, and myself) that, if they want, they can sail out with 'the old man' (Arafat). If we want to travel on the boat, there's one condition: we will have to disguise ourselves as *fedayeen*, hide our faces, and mutter an incomprehensible name to the soldiers at the symbolic checkpoint set up by the Lebanese authorities at the entrance to the quay where the *Atlantis* is due to dock. It took us three seconds to decide to go. Any journalist would have done the same.

We made our preparations in a rush, and after a sleepless night we presented ourselves, slightly embarrassed by our outsize uniforms, and with our faces hidden behind Arab *kouffiyehs*. The boat was about to leave. A good thing that we didn't have to carry Kalashnikovs as well. We would have been tripping over ourselves.

In order to get through, unrecognised, we had to wrap our heads in the *kouffiyehs* till only our eyes were showing (and in my case a pair of not-very-warlike glasses) and then stand in the August sun. And in fact, far from guaranteeing us anonymity, our get-up only drew attention to ourselves. We had hardly got out of the car when we were set upon by a horde of photographers, presumably believing that they had in their viewfinders a mysterious group of dangerous international terrorists. To find yourself 131 harassed by journalists like this is a strange experience; it's like looking into a mirror. Quite apart from the fact that one of our more mischievous colleagues might have recognised and exposed us.

We finally got through the gates. It was only as we listened to the ship's siren as the boat sailed out the port that we felt able to give a sigh of relief and breathe in the fresh sea air.

(Beirut, 30 August 1982)

Tuesday, 31 August 1982: WITH YASSER ARAFAT SAILING FROM BEIRUT

> **Where the PLO went, according to an officer of Fatah:**
> **Tunisia** 1,000 with Yasser Arafat
> **Syria** 2,500 with Georges Habash (PFLP) and Nayif Hawatmeh (PDFLP)
> **South Yemen** 1,500
> **North Yemen** 1,000
> **Sudan** 800
> **Algeria** 800

Life on board is regulated by Abu Ammar's [Arafat] appearances on deck. The 'old man' spends most of his time in his cabin, and everyone else feels free to sink into complete relaxation. But the minute he appears again, everyone stirs into life.

His commandos, the Greek crew of the ship, and the officers accompanying us – this whole little world that makes up the *Atlantis* – all try to approach him while at the same time maintaining a respectful distance. There is a lot of shyness in the admiration – one could almost say unlimited love – shown towards him. Nobody rushes in; people step out of his way. They stay close by or take a step or two towards the deckchair where he has settled himself. The Greek general who is accompanying the ship tells me that meeting Abu Ammar has been the 'proudest day of my career'.

A young Palestinian officer in his thirties tells me that he has left behind wife and children in order to follow Abu Ammar. 'The night before the departure I couldn't sleep a wink. I've already left behind my parents and brothers. They live in Egypt. The anxiety that I felt about leaving Beirut only lifted this morning, when the "old man" came up and ran his hand through my hair. At that moment I decided that I had taken the right decision, and that one day I would find my wife and child again.'

On the deck the men have overcome their shyness, and one after another they come to be photographed with their illustrious leader. He plays his part with good grace. But no sooner is the picture taken than he sinks back deep into thought, stroking his beard absent-mindedly. He seems to withdraw into himself, thinking all the time, a slight frown on his face and the air of one who is preoccupied. It is presumably this look of deep concentration that discourages the men; they don't want to butt in. But then he suddenly interrupts his internal exile, to tell a photographer that he's left his lens cap on, or to point out that a child has dropped something on deck.

The film maker in our company – who has known Yasser Arafat for a long time, and is not so easily put off – asks him point-blank to play a game of ping-pong so that he can film him. The request is gently turned down: 'No, I can't. The outside world would think "Arafat isn't worried". I don't want that. During the war I had myself photographed playing chess. That was a message to the enemy: despite the siege, the blockade and the bombardments, I wanted to show that morale was good. Today the situation is different.'

But at the same time, he readily agrees to go and play with the children around the swimming pool. The children deliberately splash him, and he splashes them back, much to the delight of anyone in sight who has a camera to hand. Soaked through, he takes one of the children in his arms and hugs and kisses him.

We return to the rear deck. A long moment passes without a word being said. All you can hear is the regular beat of the engines and the sound of the propellors churning the water. Fore and aft, and on both sides, warships accompany us at close quarters. One after another, the Palestinians come and stand with their backs to the sea, to be photographed against a backdrop of the US Sixth Fleet. Arafat still has the ping-pong ball in his hand; he plays with it absent-mindedly.

Libération: After these three months of war, this is perhaps the first real night's rest that you've had . . ? Was life in Beirut difficult?

Arafat: Yes, obviously. If we want to talk of this battle, then we have to talk of Beirut, and if we want to talk of Beirut, then we have to talk of this battle. We made history with this city. As from now, there's pre-Beirut and post-Beirut. Whatever Sharon may say, we have left Beirut with full military honours. His attempt to invade the city came to nothing. We are not leaving, now, under orders from the Israelis, but on the basis of an agreement reached between us and the Lebanese government. This is an important point.

Libération: What was the most difficult moment of this war?

Arafat: It was when the Israelis began to advance on Beirut on all fronts at once – the port, the Museum, Ouzai, the airport, the seafront – while at the same time shelling the city.

Libération: On 4 August?

Arafat: Yes. They lost a lot in the course of that offensive. And the interesting thing is that they themselves recognised this fact.

Libération: Were you expecting them to launch that attack?

Arafat: Yes, we were expecting it. But what was surprising was the resistance of the joint Palestinian and progressive forces. Yes, that was a surprise . . .

Libération: Beirut held out for more than three months, and yet no help was forthcoming from the countries of the Arab world . . .

Arafat: I expected that.

Libération: Didn't that surprise you?

Arafat: No, no, not at all. I knew that this was not going to be an easy battle. As I told you, it was a turning point. And we stood up against not only the Israelis, but also the Americans. The Americans brought into play their forces, their weapons and their influence. We shouldn't forget the number of times in the past three months that they have used their veto inside the Security Council. They have been active in the United Nations, but also elsewhere, particularly in the Arab world. They have applied the necessary pressure to prevent any real Arab reaction . . .

Libération: So the only real surprise has been the strength of the resistance in Beirut?

Arafat: There have been others. To mention just one, the fact that, despite the presence of United Nations forces, the Israelis were able to enter the UNIFIL (United Nations International Force in Lebanon) zone, and how nothing was done at the international level to counter this. How is it possible? I have to pose this question before the whole world. It was truly shameful. I can give an example: the Israelis attacked Beaufort Castle from the rear, passing through United Nations' lines. I thought that the UN flag would have been an obstacle . . .

Libération: But that was not the case . . .

Arafat: No. I regret to say that the Israelis were helped. You need only read the report prepared by the French officer commanding UNIFIL, which reveals the whole story.

Libération: Are you speaking of complicity?

Arafat: Yes, in one way or another.

Libération: What is your opinion of the way the Lebanese authorities have reacted in the course of this war?

Arafat: How can any soldier or officer of the Lebanese army accept the occupation of the palace of Baabda [the president's palace] just like that? Without any resistance? No. The Palestinians and progressive forces lost 162 martyrs, some of our best soldiers and officers, at the entry to Beirut. I'm not talking about the battle of Khalde, which lasted for five days, or the battle that followed it, alongside the airport runways at Ouzai. A hundred and sixty-two martyrs! That is military honour for you. The honour of our freedom fighters! And after that, how can I accept the excuses of the Lebanese army that didn't defend the palace of Baabda? Just like that? With no resistance? No wounded? It's shameful!

Libération: Another thing. Do you think that any progress is being made as regards an eventual dialogue between the United States and the PLO?

Arafat: No. I regret to say, no.

Libération: How do you see the period ahead, the period that starts as of tomorrow?

Arafat: I can't say anything until the meeting of the Palestinian leadership.

134 *Libération:* Do you think there is any likelihood of a meeting between you

and President Mitterrand in Greece?

Arafat: No. He's on an official visit, and I am just passing through.

Libération: Will you be coming to France, then?

Arafat: I prefer not to discuss that for the moment.

Libération: What do you expect to come out of the forthcoming Arab summit in Fez?

Arafat: This will be one of the most important meetings, for the Arabs.

Libération: And for the Palestinians?

Arafat: I would like to answer you with an Arabic poem:

> My country is still dear to me,
>> even if it oppresses me,
> And my parents are generous to me,
>> even if they show themselves greedy.

Libération: What do you think of the Fahd peace plan?

Arafat: I have already said that it could be a good starting point towards a general solution. You remember that?

Libération: Yes, of course.

Arafat: That is still my opinion.

Libération: But Israel has rejected the plan.

Arafat: Show me one single positive action that Israel has actually accepted. For example, Israel has rejected all the resolutions passed by the United Nations, despite the fact that it's the only country ever to have been created by the United Nations.

Libération: You yourself, do you accept all the UN resolutions, including the most recent?

Arafat: I am simply stating now what our Palestinian National Council has decided. We have accepted all the UN resolutions, all of them. The Israelis only accept those which allow for their aggressions, and they ignore the rest.

Libération: Do you think the Lebanon war has been more important than the 1948 war?

Arafat: Yes, without a shadow of doubt. It has been longer than all the other Arab wars put together. And the Israelis have lost more than in the previous wars. At least the battle of Beirut and the war in Lebanon have proved that nobody can annihilate the PLO. We are still here. Lebanon is not my country. It is as dear to me as any other Arab country. In fact, it is more dear, because it has shared all my trials, more than any other.

(*Atlantis*, **31 August 1982**)

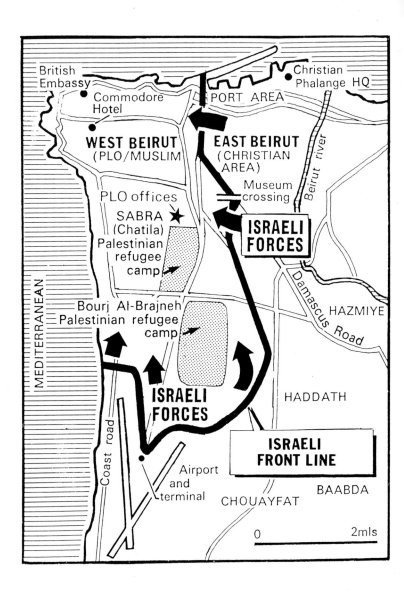

THE MASSACRE

CAROLINE TISDALL

FROM EVACUATION TO MASSACRE

1 September:
Reagan presents American peace plan proposing Palestinian self-government in association with Jordan, rejecting both a Palestinian state on the West Bank and Israeli sovereignty of it, calling for a halt to Jewish settlement in that area, and stating that future negotiations should decide the status of Jerusalem.

2 September:
Israeli cabinet unanimously rejects Reagan peace plan. Eight new settlements immediately announced.
— Sharon, Begin, Shamir and perhaps 'Major' Haddad hold secret meeting with president-elect Bashir Gemayel who is now reluctant to sign a peace treaty with Israel.

9 September:
Fez conference of Arab heads of state produces a peace plan incorporating the spirit of the Fahd peace plan, giving recognition of the PLO, the withdrawal of Israel to pre-1967 borders and the establishment of a West Bank state with Jerusalem as its capital.

13 September:
Last French contingent of the multinational peace-keeping force leaves Lebanon.

14 September:
Bashir Gemayel killed at 4.10 p.m. by bomb explosion at Phalangist headquarters. 350 members of rival Phalangist factions arrested by the SKS, the Kitaeb (Phalange) security service. Before the announcement of Gemayel's death is officially made, Begin and Sharon, without cabinet consultation, set in action 'Operation Iron Brain': it involves the occupation of West Beirut 'to prevent dangerous developments' and 'to preserve tranquillity and order'.

15 September:
At 2 a.m. Israeli Defence Force moves into West Beirut. They claim that '2,000 terrorists' are still sheltering there, some in refugee camps such as Sabra–Chatila.

THE WITNESSES: A DAY-BY-DAY ACCOUNT

Interview (by Caroline Tisdall) with Jamal, a 28-year-old Fatah leader who led the resistance in the Sabra–Chatila camp, and the report made by Dr Per Miehlumshagen, a Norwegian orthopaedic surgeon, and Dr Swee Chai Ang, a British orthopaedic surgeon, who were both working in Gaza Hospital in the middle of the camp. Dr Ang, aged 32, formerly of St Thomas' Hospital, London, went to Lebanon as a Christian Aid volunteer in mid-August. She later testified in Jerusalem to the Kahan Commission of Enquiry.

Jamal: After the evacuation people gradually started to come back to the camps. During the war and the heaviest bombardments most of them had been sheltering in flats and empty schools outside the camps, in terrible conditions and sometimes 20 to a room, while the fighters stayed in the camps. So it was a relief to come 'home', and a relief that the bombardments had stopped. But we were numbed by the devastation and the uncertainty of the future. There was the feeling that even if we found the money to rebuild our houses, they would be destroyed again. At the same time, we had built up those homes over 34 years, so everyone began searching for their things under the rubble and trying to recreate at least the shape of a room. Water was a terrible problem, with dust from the rubble getting into everything.

My own home was in the centre of Chatila: one large room and two small ones with a courtyard and a beautiful acacia tree. There are nine of us, my mother and father, who has worked as a radiologist in one of the hospitals for the past 25 years, and my brothers and sisters. My family is from Haifa, but this was the house I was born in, which we were rebuilding with breeze blocks.

At a meeting of the camp committee ten days before the massacre, we had decided to lay down our personal weapons. As you know, the PLO handed over its heavy weapons at the time of the evacuation, but we still had the Kalashnikovs with which we have defended the camps since 1969. We surrendered them to the Lebanese National Movement. It was a hard decision but we took it for several reasons. After the election of Bashir Gemayel, the Lebanese army came into the camps searching for arms, and found the underground store in Sabra. We knew that if they found more large caches there could be reprisals. That was why, when we realised a massacre was happening in Chatila and tried to organise resistance, we could only find one rocket launcher, 5 rockets, and 15 Kalashnikovs, all of which had

pages 140 and 141: map of Sabra–Chatila camp based on drawing by Jamal (interviewed PLO resistance leader) 139

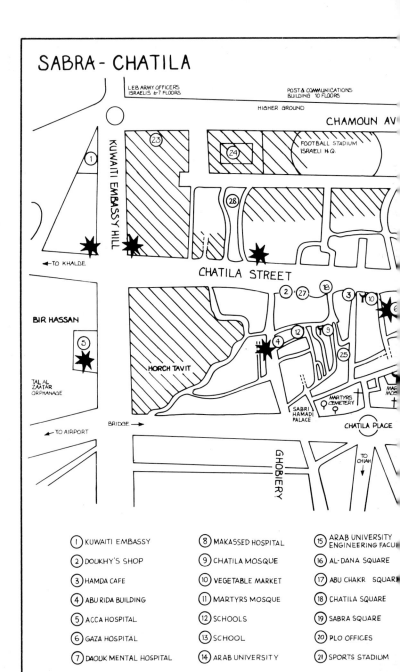

SABRA - CHATILA

LEB ARMY OFFICERS
ISRAELIS 6-7 FLOORS

POST & COMMUNICATIONS
BUILDING 10 FLOORS

HIGHER GROUND

CHAMOUN AV

KUWAITI EMBASSY HILL

23

24

FOOTBALL STADIUM
ISRAELI H.Q.

1

28

←TO KHALDE

CHATILA STREET

2 27

18

3 10

BIR HASSAN

5

4

12

9

6

25

HORCH TAVIT

MARTYRS
CEMETERY

MAR
MOS

TAL AL
ZAATAR
ORPHANAGE

SABRI
HAMADI
PALACE

CHATILA PLACE

←TO AIRPORT

BRIDGE →

GHOBIERY

TO
CHIAH
↓

① KUWAITI EMBASSY	⑧ MAKASSED HOSPITAL	⑮ ARAB UNIVERSITY ENGINEERING FACU
② DOUKHY'S SHOP	⑨ CHATILA MOSQUE	⑯ AL-DANA SQUARE
③ HAMDA CAFE	⑩ VEGETABLE MARKET	⑰ ABU CHAKR SQUAR
④ ABU RIDA BUILDING	⑪ MARTYRS MOSQUE	⑱ CHATILA SQUARE
⑤ ACCA HOSPITAL	⑫ SCHOOLS	⑲ SABRA SQUARE
⑥ GAZA HOSPITAL	⑬ SCHOOL	⑳ PLO OFFICES
⑦ DAOUK MENTAL HOSPITAL	⑭ ARAB UNIVERSITY	㉑ SPORTS STADIUM

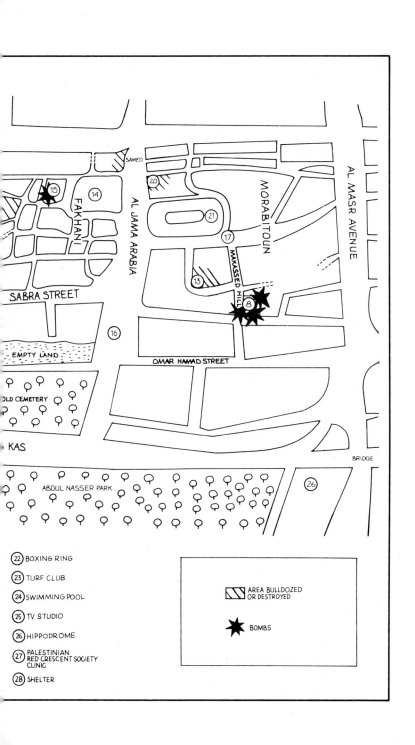

SAMED

⑮ FAKHANI ⑭

AL JAMA ARABIA

⑳

㉑ ⑰

MORABITOUN

AL MASR AVENUE

SABRA STREET

MAKASSED HILL

⑬

⑧

⑯

EMPTY LAND

OMAR HAMAD STREET

OLD CEMETERY

KAS

BRIDGE

ABDUL NASSER PARK

㉖

㉒ BOXING RING

㉓ TURF CLUB

㉔ SWIMMING POOL

㉕ TV STUDIO

㉖ HIPPODROME

㉗ PALESTINIAN RED CRESCENT SOCIETY CLINIC

㉘ SHELTER

AREA BULLDOZED OR DESTROYED

BOMBS

been greased, wrapped in sacking and plastic and buried because we didn't expect to use them. We didn't even have time or petrol to clean off the grease so, when it came to it, all we had were about 45 men and boys trying to protect Chatila with 15 boiling-hot greasy guns and one rocket launcher.

But the main reason for disarming was that although the future looked uncertain we didn't expect war to come again. We felt that the PLO had kept the terms of the Habib agreement in evacuating, and we had to put our trust in the multinational peace-keeping force to protect us. They should never have left so early. After that we had to depend on the Lebanese National Movement. Meanwhile on the TVs we were running off car batteries (there was no electricity), we could hear Bashir Gemayel beginning to talk about the Palestinians: how they must pay their bills for 14 years' electricity and so on . . .

Dr Ang and Dr Miehlumshagen: We were working in Gaza Hospital during the evacuation. During the war it had been bombed and lost its top two floors, so it was now a nine-storey building. There was no running water, and only three hours of generated power a day during which we carried out operations. The cases we were treating were mostly old injuries from the war and the bombardments which needed resetting or amputation. By 13 September we were running like a normal hospital in the sense that we had secure water and electricity.

Tuesday, 14 September 1982

Jamal: At 5.51 p.m. we heard the news that Bashir Gemayel had been injured, on the Phalangist radio, 'The Voice of Lebanon'. At 7.15 the newscaster's voice was deep and sad instead of the usual shouting. At 11 p.m. the death of Gemayel was announced, and programmes replaced with classical music.

Wednesday, 15 September 1982

Dr A & Dr M: Between 5 and 5.30 a.m. flights of Israeli airplanes came in from the sea in the direction of the camps. We heard the news of Bashir Gemayel's death on the radio. At Gaza Hospital an emergency meeting was held and all operations cancelled. The director, acting from experience, felt this might be the beginning of another war. The first explosions were heard at 8 a.m. in the southern region of the camp. The shelling was continuous and by midday had been intense in a radius of five kilometres from the hospital, as witnessed from the roof. Only walking casualties were treated that day as roads leading to

The search for the dead: mourning women in Sabra-Chatila

the hospital were closed to ambulances.

The shelling came nearer and nearer and by about 4 p.m. the zone of shelling was thought to be less than a kilometre away from the hospital. News arrived that Israeli troops had surrounded and were getting past Acca Hospital at the southern limit of Chatila. By nightfall the shelling gradually diminished, but the camp was lit by flares. It was clear to us that we were entirely surrounded.

Jamal: At 5.30 a.m. a friend from Sabra came to our house in Chatila. We went together up Sabra Street to the Engineering Building of the Arab University – which had been bombed in the war – to see what was happening. I was still half asleep so when I saw six soldiers hiding in an entrance opposite the faculty, I thought they must be the Lebanese army . . . When I realised they were 'our uncle's son' – that's what we call our enemy – I was astonished. They were only three yards away, listening to their radios, and looked very frightened. Further south down Chamoun Avenue there were two tanks and a jeep. We couldn't understand how or when they got here and all within less than six hours of the announcement of Gemayel's death.

We went on through to West Beirut to check out what was happening and try to get help, but in vain. We realised that Begin was saying that there were still 2,000 'terrorists' in the camp, and that meant they could come and kill the men aged 14–60. We returned to the camp and, because it was unprotected and we had no guns, there were only two choices at that point: to stay or to go. I would say that about 5 per cent of the men left then. They left because they were afraid, but what kind of decision can you make when you haven't the weapons to defend yourself?

From 8.30 a.m. there was shelling and sniping from the sports stadium which is on higher ground and is the emplacement used by the Lebanese army in 1973. They were using 155mm howitzers and 800-type high velocity rifles. From here and the Kuwaiti Embassy in the south-west corner, they could control and cut off the road connecting Sabra and Chatila at the level of the Hamda Cafe. They began to shell the Mukhalalati building by the cafe in Chatila Square, the only six-floor building in the area, presumably because they thought we could use it for sniping.

That night the camp was lit with flares which were shot up every 30 seconds or so and cast a strange magnesium light. I went back home after midnight, and my father and I persuaded my mother, sisters and grandmother to go to the shelter near the school. My father and I stayed and I slept for a couple of hours on the sofa. That was strange – sleeping there when from one destroyed room of the house you could see right through to the stadium where the shelling was coming from. That's when I lost my documents – you know how careful we have to be about those – and mine prove I was born in Lebanon . . . Anyway,

Finding the dead: mourning women in Sabra–Chatila

I left them under that sofa in an expensive leather bag my brother gave me, with my address book and favourite photos. Nothing political – all that had been burnt well before.

Thursday, 16 September 1982

Dr A & Dr M: We were woken about 5.30 a.m. again by aircraft flying across at low height. Shelling and explosions continued after that. In addition, there were distinct gunshot noises (rifles).

Casualties poured into the hospital from mid-morning most of whom were suffering from high-velocity gunshot wounds. It was evident from the casualties brought in then that the gunmen had gone into the homes of the people in Sabra–Chatila camp and started shooting them in their homes. We were told by the casualties that these gunmen were not Israelis, but Lebanese with a Baalbek accent.

The medical team, then comprising two surgeons, two anaesthetists and five residents, worked non-stop. About 30 very seriously wounded were brought in who died while still receiving individual treatment. About 25 to 30 patients were in good enough condition to be operated upon. About 80–100 wounded were treated in casualty. Another 30 or so patients were transferred to Makassed hospital as the workload became unmanageable.

Meanwhile, the shooting and shelling continued outside. By nightfall, an estimated 2,000 refugees had flocked into the hospital seeking refuge, sleeping all over the hospital staircase and floors. Throughout the night, the camps surrounding Gaza Hospital were lit up, and shooting continued.

Jamal: There was heavy shelling all day which lasted till Friday morning. In the early morning we held a meeting in the camp office which is where people usually gather when there is an emergency. That's when we realised that there were two things we had to achieve. Firstly we had to protect the people in the camp by trying to find safe places for them to gather. At the same time we had to organise resistance: we had to gather the fighters left in the camp and try to find some weapons. That meant going round the houses for guns that the old people had hidden since they were mostly too frightened to come out. That's how we ended up with the 15 greasy guns and the rocket launcher between 45 of us – some of us only 16 years old. At that point we concentrated our resistance. We split up into small groups, each to try to defend the spots they came from and the alleys they knew best: the southern, eastern and western edges, Chatila Place and towards the bridge on the airport road. Some of the groups didn't even have a gun. It was horrible and confusing to the point where you just stopped thinking. It happened so fast: suddenly the enemy was there and the houses

Digging out the mutilated dead

were collapsing.

You might wonder why so many people stayed in their houses and didn't risk the sniping and run northwards. But inside the camp the shelling and sniping seemed to be coming from everywhere, so where would they run to? Anyway, they were sick of running.

I went up to Sabra to find a man I thought might have some guns, but it was useless – he wasn't even in the camp. In Sabra I saw that the resistance there amounted to 16 or so very young fighters with six or seven guns who were trying to hold the area in front of the mental hospital in Daouk by Sabra Square.

Back in Chatila they were bombing the Abu Rida building near the elementary schools. It was a three-storey white building and some friends of mine lived there. I tried to cross to it but realised that it was impossible – the road was completely controlled by sniper fire perhaps from the Turf Club near the stadium. That afternoon a Lebanese army officer outside the camp in Chiah destroyed an Israeli tank which was coming in from Chatila Place on the east. I suppose he felt that in spite of everything he must do something. After that the tanks withdrew on that side.

At 3.30 I stopped for coffee with a friend. Up to this point I just thought the Israelis were invading. I didn't realise till then that a massacre was happening. But then I was told about the old men and I understood. Five of the elders had met in a house and decided of their own accord to go out to the Israelis and say, 'We have no fighters here. Stop the bombing. You are killing our women and children and old people.' One of them was the father of a doctor in Gaza Hospital, Dr Saad. They walked out of the south entrance with a white flag. Four were shot and the fifth came back shaking and pale and ran towards the north hardly able to speak. Many people were injured running north.

On Thursday the flares over the camp began at 5.30 p.m. because although the horizon was still light, the narrow spaces between the houses and alleys were getting dark. There were aircraft dropping light bombs too. The night was like day.

The next few hours were terrible. I saw people running in panic to the small mosque, Chatila Mosque. They were taking shelter there because apart from being a sanctuary it was also built with a strong steel structure. Inside were 26 women and children – some of them had horrible injuries. There was an old woman of 70 with blood pouring from a wound in her throat but whose love of life still kept her on her feet. They were crying out to be taken to hospital. By the Hamda cafe I found a dark blue Austin Allegro and a really brave man who said it belonged to him. We couldn't get the car down the alley because of the rubble so we had to carry people from the mosque to it. But the 70-year-old woman got there on her own. All those people rushed to that one car to be taken but we had to hold them

Some of the 1,500 victims

back until we carried a rather fat woman with stomach injuries to it and put her on the back seat. But then it was impossible to control the others – they all piled on top of her. I went with the car to try to bring back an ambulance.

At that moment, it was 6 p.m. – a woman running with a child on the street told me the Kitaeb (Phalangist militia) were coming through the alleys in the south-west opposite the swimming pool. They had reached the shelter and killed everyone in it. She said that an Israeli soldier was accompanying a Kitaeb whom she recognised as a Christian from his accent. While the Kitaeb was killing the people in the shelter, the Israeli shouted '*ruch, ruch*' to her – that means 'run away' in Arabic but the accent was clear to her. Maybe he was shouting that because the Israelis feel they are more civilised than those they use to do their work.

It took ages to get back to the mosque with the ambulance because so many people were rushing northwards to Gaza Hospital. By now the snipers could reach right up to the hospital along Chatila Street and there was complete chaos. Then I remembered my family and tried to get to our house. That was difficult. They had bombed around it so much that journalists afterwards thought it had been damaged in the air raids of the war. It was as if they thought there was a cannon there. By then I was crazy. I was shouting to the women that they should fight back with knives and sticks.

People were shouting, 'They've reached Doukhy's.' Doukhy's shop sold gas on the corner near the three-storey building, so it was like a landmark. They'd killed Doukhy and his family. To get this far they had used the smallest alleys. I feel they must have been led in by some of the former Lebanese camp dwellers who went to south Lebanon and joined Haddad. It wasn't possible to monitor everything that went on in the camp in 'normal' times, and maybe the area had been infiltrated. Many Lebanese camp dwellers were killed down in the south-east of the camp opposite Acca Hospital, in the part we call Horsh Tavit. In a single family, the Makdaads, 82 members were killed on Thursday alone. Then Horsh Tavit was bulldozed flat.

In the main street, the enemy had now occupied the building with a cafe opposite Doukhy's and were sniping along the left and centre of Chatila Street. For a time it was still possible to move along the right of the street, but by 8.30 they succeeded in controlling all of it entirely, right up to the al-Dana Mosque and Gaza Hospital. So people began to use the side roads, moving up to behind the vegetable supermarket and so on. Those are the little paths that only Chatila people know. They were safer too because in Ghobiery the Amal had destroyed four Israeli tanks, stopping them moving in from the east.

Four of us were trying to hold the area round the TV studio which had been bombed almost as much as the stadium. We were in a side street and my cousin had the rocket launcher opposite. We were

trying to stop them and at the same time save rockets because we only had five. We tried and failed: when we shot they replied with inertia rockets and we were afraid because there were civilians all around. My cousin is very young and was looking a bit frightened and pale so I crossed over the street and asked him to hand the grenade launcher over to his friend. I don't even know who he was because he was wearing the *kouffiyeh*.

Without thinking I asked my cousin where his mother – my aunt – was. When he said 'I don't know' I found myself just acting by instinct. I rushed back towards Chatila Mosque. There were a few people in there, an old man and a couple of fighters outside. All they said was, 'They are killing everyone.' I reached our house through the back alley. The main door was open. I called. My father answered. I told him to be quiet. My father tried to lock the door. My father, grandmother, uncle and cousin were all hiding there, under the place we used to store water on the roof.

This part is the most difficult to tell. My father said the rest of the family were in the shelter. I knew they had to get out of there. So I asked my grandmother to go to the shelter to tell them to go. I asked her because in spite of all I'd seen I couldn't believe they would shoot my grandmother. But I knew they would shoot me and I felt I had to continue in this hell. To make it worse, my grandmother is a little deaf and I had to talk loudly to her while we could hear the enemy in our neighbour's house, shouting at him: 'Come here you son of a bitch.' They were so close. We heard the neighbour shout 'But I'm Mohammed Nabusi. I'm the brother of the wrestling champion' – as if that would make any difference. I don't know why he said that. But after that there was silence. They killed him. He was a good man.

After that I went with my grandmother towards the mosque and she went to get the rest of the family from the shelter. They took five minutes to come a few metres. Then they realised they'd forgotten my baby cousin's bottle. The panic was all very strange. I said I'd go and get the bottle. My aunt said she would. In the end my aunt and uncle both insisted on going for the bottle while I stayed holding the baby. I suppose these things happened because we felt so trapped. You could hardly think. Anyway after that I took them up to Gaza Hospital, and then I joined the fighters nearby because it was the only suitable spot to attempt resistance.

Yet within a quarter of an hour I came back to the same area, this time with two fighters. It seems like a contradiction, but I was drawn back. We moved down past the Sabri Hammadi Palace, towards the *ashbal*, the training ground for boys. Then a girl came running, shouting 'They are here.' They shot her, and the girl who was running behind her. My friend Sami ran to pick them up, and they shot him too. One girl was dead. We carried the other girl to Gaza Hospital and she survived. But Sami died on the way. It was 10 p.m.

Palestinians return to the wreckage of
their homes in Bourj al-Brajneh

That night the entire southern entrance was bulldozed. We heard the noise of the engines working and thought they were tanks. That's where the Makdaad family was killed. I was sure then that the entire east side of the camp was empty of people. They killed everyone they found, but the point is the *way* they killed them. They found a mother holding a five year-old. They took the child and pretended they were about to kill him, not just once but two or three times. Then they killed him and told her he would have been a *fedayeen* one day. They said, 'We don't need to kill you – you'll die with this memory.' There was the daughter of Abu Diab who was 15. They tied her hands and legs and did everything that men can to her. Then they drove an iron bar up her and killed her. There was Fahd, an 18-year-old Syrian whose head was split open with an axe in front of his mother. There was Abu Brahim who survived – he was one of the fighters, but he lives with the memory that his mother, sister and brothers were killed and that his pregnant wife had the baby cut out of her and was then killed. They must have been crazed to do things like that. After the massacre we found the place some of them had stayed in that night, among the breeze blocks we had brought for rebuilding. Piles of lager cans, and two syringes.

Friday, 17 September 1982

Dr A & Dr M: People wounded by gunshot continued to be brought in. At about 10 a.m. the hospital administrator left the hospital in an attempt to make contact with the International Red Cross, appealing for more medical workers, and relief for the refugees, and to get the foreign medical workers registered, as well as to make radio contact with the Israeli Defence Forces to protect the foreign medical staff and to control the assassins now rampant in the refugee camp. The hospital administrator returned about midday and told the foreign medical workers that something very terrible was about to happen. She then proceeded to instruct the refugees already present in the hospital that the hospital was no longer a safe area, and that at any time the Phalangist Kitaeb or, even worse, the Haddads, might move in. The 2,000 or so refugees were evacuated rapidly. She then proceeded to instruct the remaining handful of Palestinian personnel (two residents, some nurses and technicians) to leave while there was still time. By 4.30 p.m. she came to the foreign medical team, and told them that she too had to leave and that although she herself was Lebanese she was in personal danger, as the hospital was infiltrated.

The hospital quietened down that night, although shootings were still taking place outside the camps. Patients were now beginning to

Lebanese army rounding up young Palestinians whose documents are allegedly not in order

discharge themselves, and some were carried out by their own families.

Jamal: From 2 a.m. to 6 a.m. it was calm, just some shooting here and there, and the flares again. They use their technology to psychological effect and we were sure by now it would be *terra rasa* for us. I was in the Gaza Hospital with my family. At 6.30 an old man and his wife were sniped at just outside by the vegetable market, she in the leg and he in the stomach, so we put up notices written on bits of cardboard box on the corners of the vegetable market, 'Beware of snipers'.

At 7.15 a.m. in Sabra Place we heard them calling through loud-speakers. They were telling us to give up and come out of our houses. They were saying the Israeli Defence Force is a peaceful army come to protect the Palestinians from the Christians. All through Friday, Saturday and Sunday they were calling people together to go to the stadium to have their documents stamped.

I left Chatila and reached a friend's house in Chiah at 7.45 a.m. On the way I crossed Chatila Place and went near to the Museum crossing where I had served in the war. The traffic was coming and going and nobody seemed to care whether anything was going on. I asked someone if anything had happened in Chiah. They said nothing had, and that the people in Chiah did not want firing in their district. After three hours spent trying to get help I went back to Chatila, and found my family had left Gaza Hospital.

Then I went north to the Abu Chakr district, and found my family. I was very tired and slept there with all the other families in a wrecked entrance to a building.

Saturday, 18 September 1982

Dr A & Dr M: At 6.45 a.m. an American nurse spotted some soldiers outside Gaza Hospital and a doctor was sent down to negotiate the situation. The soldiers identified themselves as 'Lebanese Forces' and their officers requested that all foreign medical personnel be assembled to be taken for interrogation. A nurse and a medical student were left behind to look after those in intensive care. The rest of the team was soon passed on to other troops who escorted them to the courtyard of the UNICEF building (about 10 minutes walk) to be interrogated. On both sides of the road groups of women and children were rounded up by soldiers (not wearing Lebanese uniform, but just green military clothes, with green baseball-type caps). We estimated there may well have been 800 to 1,000 women and children.

Large bulldozers were at work tearing down partly shelled buildings and burying bodies within these buildings into the rubble. A woman tried to pass her baby into a foreign doctor's arms, but was forced by the soldiers to take the baby back.

In the courtyard of the UNICEF building, our papers were checked and questions regarding our political affiliations were asked. Most of the soldiers identified themselves as Christians. We were held in the courtyard for more than an hour and it was about 9.30 a.m. when we were taken out of the courtyard to the Israeli headquarters on a road parallel to Sabra Street.

In the presence of an Israeli film crew, assurances were given that everything would be done to keep our patients safe, to help to get us out, and to get food and water to the hospital. Two male doctors and one male nurse were allowed to go back to Gaza to help out, but the rest of the team were taken by two Israeli jeeps to the American Embassy and dropped there. When more of us wanted to go back to Gaza Hospital, the Israeli soldiers warned us that it was highly unsafe, and hence only three were escorted back.

The nurse who was left in Gaza Hospital testified that half an hour after we had left, continuous machine-gun firing lasting 20 minutes to half an hour was heard, accompanied by screaming of women and children. After that, everything quietened down. The time was then between 7.30 a.m. and 8.30 a.m.

A BBC correspondent who arrived, about 9.30 a.m., at Gaza Hospital said that heaps of dead bodies piled on top of each other, in groups of ten or more, lined Sabra Street. Most of these dead were women and young children. A Canadian film crew arriving around 10 a.m. or so filmed Sabra Street with numerous dead bodies piled on top of each other on either side of the road. When we were shown the video, we could identify some of them as the people who were being rounded up by the troops on either side of Sabra Street when we passed at 7 a.m. that morning. Journalists arriving later saw bulldozers at work tearing down buildings and burying bodies in the rubble. The patients and doctors, nurses (foreign) were later evacuated by the International Committee of the Red Cross (ICRC).

Sunday, 19 September 1982

Jamal: I woke at 5.30 to find my father had gone. My mother said he'd returned to Chatila to find the bag with our family's documents in it, our '48 documents without which one would 'disappear' immediately. I knew he was crazy to go back then and I really broke down. I was shouting and banging my head against the wall.

But he survived and told us what happened. He got back to our house, and found the bag and filled another with some eggs and tomatoes. Then outside the wreck of the Palestinian Red Crescent clinic in Chatila Street he'd been told to stop there by a Haddad man who marched him 10 metres before a Phalangist came up with a gun and told him to drop the bags. My father kept saying they had our documents in them, but he had to leave them. They marched him with hundreds of other people down to the southern entrance of the camp. There the men were separated from the women who all began 157 to recite the Koran, preparing for the worst. The men were marched up the Kuwaiti Embassy Hill and a bomb exploded. The Egyptian in front of my father was killed and the injured were left lying there. Some ran. Then an Israeli lorry came and loaded them up and took them to their headquarters in the stadium. One of the officers who spoke good Palestinian Arabic asked who was from Chatila and Sabra. My father was one of the lucky ones who was released. Maybe he was lucky to be arrested – most of the mass shootings in the camp were going on at 7.30.

We did not return to the camp until Tuesday.

Dr A & Dr M: Members of the medical team, including Dr Miehlumshagen, were able to return to Sabra–Chatila camp in the morning. Dead bodies were seen everywhere; whole families had been shot together, and in one particular case, there was the body of a man (presumably the father) trying to use his own body to shield his wife and children from the assassins.

The total number of dead people was estimated by the ICRC at that time as 1,500.

We tried to return to Sabra–Chatila camp in the afternoon but found the whole camp sealed off by Lebanese tanks and troops. We also witnessed 10 to 15 Israeli tanks withdrawing from the scene.

WHY?

Jamal: We do not know how many died. The Red Cross said 1,500 at the time, and then there were at least 900 who were driven off and never seen again. Some dead bodies were found along the roads going east and to the mountains.

You can't separate the war and the massacre. I believe they were trying to set a terrible example for the other Arab countries, to prevent the other Arab peoples ever accepting the Palestinians as an organised force in their midst, and to show them what would happen if they did. They wanted us to run to Syria and be simply absorbed, not organised. I think they failed in this. All through the three months of the war the ordinary Lebanese people helped and protected us. Even at the time of the massacre the people of West Beirut were finding shelter for us: by the Sunday they had found a flat for my family.

Psychologically it is clear what they were trying to do to us. We were trapped like animals in that camp, and that is how they have always tried to show us to the world. They wanted us to believe it ourselves. They wanted to terrify and traumatise us, to leave us with memories we can never forget. Perhaps in that they have succeeded, but only as long as we remain unarmed.

As fighters they wanted to humiliate us. They couldn't beat us armed so they beat us unarmed: 'the hordes came when the fighters left' is what we say to that. The experience of being unable to defend even my own family when the whole camp is my family has left me confused and very angry. But as a fighter I don't have a sense of failure because I feel that as a resistance we were able to do much more than we thought we could with limited and unimpressive weapons.

Before the war they said we were terrorists and that we were training terrorists in our camps. Everyone who knows us knows we were fighters you could trust, and that we were trying to build a progressive mentality. Why didn't they write that every day? It's related to philosophy: when you are building something and the enemy comes and destroys this thing again and again, it means you are on the right road, however long it may be.